Defending an Economic Superpower

Reassessing the U.S.-Japan Security Alliance

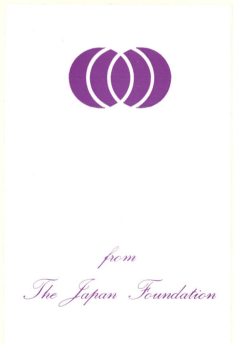

from

The Japan Foundation

Defending an Economic Superpower

Reassessing the U.S.-Japan Security Alliance

Tetsuya Kataoka
and Ramon H. Myers

Westview Press
BOULDER, SAN FRANCISCO, & LONDON

Westview Special Studies on East Asia

Copyright © 1989 by Westview Press, Inc.

Published in 1989 in the United States of America by Westview Press, Inc., 5500 Central Avenue, Boulder, Colorado 80301, and in the United Kingdom by Westview Press, Inc., 13 Brunswick Centre, London WC1N 1AF, England

Library of Congress Cataloging-in-Publication Data
Kataoka, Tetsuya.
    Defending an economic superpower : reassessing the U.S.-Japan
security alliance / Tetsuya Kataoka and Ramon H. Myers.
        p. cm. — (Westview special studies on East Asia)
    Bibliography: p.
    Includes index.
    ISBN 0-8133-0818-6
    1. Japan—National security. 2. Japan—Military relations—United
States. 3. United States—Military relations—Japan. 4. United
States—Military policy. I. Title. II. Series.
UA845.K366 1989
355'.033052—dc19   88-27001
                                                                      CIP

Printed and bound in the United States of America

10   9   8   7   6   5   4   3   2

Contents

Tables and Illustrations

Acknowledgments

We are grateful for the U.S.-Japan Friendship Commission's financial support of this study. Our research was also supported by a grant from the U.S. Department of Defense. This financial support made it possible for us to visit Japan, conduct interviews, gather relevant information, and hold a seminar in Tokyo (June 1986), where some two dozen Japanese defense experts critiqued an early draft of this study.

Tetsuya Kataoka
Ramon H. Myers

1

Posing the Problem

By 1988, a new argument began to receive serious consideration in the United States: American security commitments throughout the globe could no longer be maintained at their current levels without a substantial sharing of that burden with allies.

We also believe the American economy has been growing more slowly than other advanced economies and probably cannot support American security commitments in the near future at the same level as in the recent past. This perception that America's relative economic decline does not augur well for the support of her global security commitments can be found in many recent writings.

Paul Kennedy's sweeping *tour d'horizon* narrating how Austria, England, the United States, and other countries expanded their spheres of influence, only to see them decline, makes the case that when a country's economic capabilities begin to decline, its sphere of influence can no longer be maintained by military power.[1] David P. Calleo's probing analysis of the tensions emerging within the Western European alliance in recent decades because of increasing costs also shows that within the next decade or so some new cooperative arrangement between European states will most likely emerge to maintain Western Europe's security, thus replacing American dominance in NATO.[2] Samuel P. Huntington's recent essay in *Foreign Affairs* describes how the gap between America's security commitments and her ability to maintain those commitments could be corrected by substitute arrangements, but only if allies exert greater effort to share the burden, such as paying a defense tax to the United States.[3]

In March 1988, the Center for Strategic and International Studies in Washington assembled a bipartisan group of business and government leaders, headed by William E. Brock, the former special trade representative and secretary of labor in the Reagan administration. The group offered these central findings:

- Although the U.S. economy is still the most powerful in the world, unless foreign trade and productivity improve, its standing relative to other major economies will continue to decline.

- U.S. industry is still at the forefront of innovation, but other countries have narrowed the gap, and some are even surpassing it in many manufacturing applications.
- America's security obligations have remained unchanged in recent decades, while economic competition with her allies has intensified, thus weakening America's competitive edge.[4]

The conclusion, based on the above findings, was that the United States can no longer afford to maintain its current security commitments.

Whatever the reasons for the decline of the United States in its relative economic standing with other countries—a falling saving rate, sagging productivity, or a slowing pace of innovation—new economic competition from abroad has jolted many in the United States to reassess America's economic capabilities. The new economic competition, of course, has originated from broad changes in the world's production structure, especially in the Pacific Basin. By the 1960s, Japan had begun restructuring its economy, and she was followed in the 1970s and 1980s by other countries in the Pacific Basin doing the same thing. The surge in gross national product and foreign trade in that part of the world inspired some observers to predict that the next century would be the "Pacific Century."[5]

Today, Japan's gross national product is more than 50 percent that of the United States, and her economy is growing slightly faster. The total exports of the four Little Tigers—Hong Kong, Singapore, the Republic of China on Taiwan, and South Korea—are projected to reach 80 percent of Japan's in 1989. Given the booming economies of Malaysia, Thailand, and the People's Republic of China, when the twenty-first century begins, the region of North and Northeast Asia could well account for more than 25 percent of the world's total production, versus less than 30 percent for North America. The comparable numbers now are 20 percent and 28 percent, respectively.[6] These developments have only increased America's trade imbalance with the Pacific Basin.

In 1981, the U.S. deficit with Asia's four newly industrialized countries of South Korea, the Republic of China, Hong Kong, and Singapore was $6.1 billion; it reached $37 billion in 1987, or 22 percent of the total U.S. trade deficit.[7] But it was the economic dominance of Japan in Asia and its emergence as a new world economic superpower that eventually focused our concern on the U.S.-Japanese relationship. While drawing 23 percent of all imports from the United States, Japan ran a whopping bilateral trade surplus in 1987 of $51.4 billion.[8] But that figure was only $6.9 billion in 1980, and Japan had a deficit of $459 million in 1975. Indeed, dramatic change in U.S.-Japanese economic relations had occurred in the 1980s.[9]

By 1986, some severely criticized Japan for its unfair economic policies, which were supposed to be undermining America's economic competitive edge.

For example, Karel G. van Wolferen urged American policy-makers to take strong action to force the Japanese to change their trading practices.[10] But Japan was being criticized not only for its economic policies. In the spring of 1986, there appeared a sharp attack on Japan that criticized it for paying too little for its defense and that urged Japan to do more to help the United States prevent the balance of power in the Pacific Basin from shifting toward the Soviet Union. The attack, an advertisement in the *New York Times,* was signed by scholars and policy-makers from the United States, the Republic of Korea, and even Japan. It called upon Japan to "do more to protect its coasts, straits, sea lanes and airspace from Soviet domination." To that end, the advertisement asked that Japan make "a substantial increase in defense spending."[11]

By the mid-1980s, the U.S. government was running the largest budget deficit in its history, and the United States had become the world's largest debtor country. A flood of journal articles and newspaper editorials discussed why Japan spent so little for defense and how Japan could do more to help the United States defend the Pacific Basin.[12] For almost twenty years Japan had spent slightly less than 1 percent of its gross national product for its defense, as compared to the United States' 7.1 percent in 1972, 5.4 percent in 1980, and 6.9 percent in 1987.[13] Why should the United States outspend the Japanese some five to seven times for defense while going deeper into debt?

Japan's not spending more for defense and her allegedly unfair ways of doing business with the United States were certainly the two main reasons why relations between Japan and the United States soured in the 1980s. Not since the end of World War II have relations between the two allies been so poor. These two issues are now even more relevant to the new debate in the United States over whether America can defend the globe if its economy is faltering and social problems are worsening.[14] Although some argue that the U.S. economy is still healthy and will readily grow in the coming decades, others are already reassessing America's security alliance with its allies to ask whether those alliances are being managed to the best interests of the United States. Melvyn Krauss and David P. Calleo, for example, have found the NATO security arrangement flawed and have suggested that the U.S. contribution to NATO be reduced and that our NATO allies do more for Europe's defense.

The Scope of This Study

Our study reassesses the U.S.-Japan security relationship to determine how Japan can do more for its defense, reduce America's spending for Japan's and Asia's security, and yet preserve the peace in that region. We raise six questions about the U.S.-Japan security relationship and try to provide answers from the historical record.

The first question asks how Japan and the United States agreed to a security alliance in the first place. Chapter 2 reviews the origin of the postwar U.S.-

Japanese security relations that allowed Japan to concentrate on developing its economy while enjoying a "free ride." This historical review covers the developments from the early years of the American occupation of Japan up to 1975. Our account shows that the American occupation authorities drew up a new constitution for Japan that contained the famous Article IX, by which Japan pledged to "forever renounce war as a sovereign right of the nation and the threat or use of force as a means of settling international disputes." But then the United States reversed itself in 1951 and proposed that Japan enter into a new security treaty that allowed America to have military bases in Japan in return for protecting Japan. Shigeru Yoshida, prime minister from October 1948 to October 1954, was the political leader who opted for the strategy under which Japan would accept the new constitution and the security treaty, thus giving the country free rein to devote all its energies to economic development.[15] This policy became known as the Yoshida strategy.

Although this strategy worked successfully until the mid-1970s, continued Soviet military expansion and that country's invasion of Afghanistan in the late 1970s forced the United States to begin building up its arms and to demand that its allies do the same. Late in the Carter administration, as well as during the Reagan administration, American officials strongly pressed the Japanese government to accelerate defense spending and cooperate more closely with the United States in the Northeast Pacific. Because of these external pressures on Japan, the Yoshida strategy was modified, and Japan began a moderate arms expansion. Chapter 2 describes the refinement of the Yoshida strategy under these new circumstances.

By the late 1970s, the U.S.-Japan security alliance also came under careful scrutiny by Japan's policy-makers and leaders, which brings us to our second question: Why did the Japanese reexamine the U.S.-Japan security alliance, and what strategy did they finally adopt by the mid-1980s that still remains in place? Chapter 3 answers these questions by reviewing the different points of view being expressed in the media about the perceived threats to Japan's security and how to deal with them. For the first time, many Japanese are openly expressing a concern about the new expansion of Soviet military power in the Pacific Basin and a possible U.S. withdrawal from that region.

By 1978, the Soviet Union had fortified Soviet bases in Japan's Northern Territories, then occupied by the Soviet Union. That November, the Soviet Union concluded a treaty of friendship with Vietnam and acquired basing rights in Vietnam. By 1980, the Soviet Union had turned Cam Ranh Bay into an important military base.[16] Soviet aircraft operated from Da Nang, and Soviet diesel-powered submarines were photographed in Cam Ranh Bay. This new military thrust by Moscow gave Soviet leaders the opportunity to control the sea routes linking the Pacific with the Indian Ocean and beyond, if the United States did decide to retreat from Asia.

Many interpreted these developments as an adverse shift in the balance of power for Japan and believed that she should quickly strengthen her defenses. In the early 1980s, the United States began urging Japan to expand its Self-Defense Forces and to cooperate more closely with American air and naval forces to monitor and defend the sea-lanes within 1,000 nautical miles of Japan. Yet the United States was really unwilling to ask Japan to do any more than that, fearing adverse Asian reaction. Therefore, the United States asked Japan to increase spending for foreign aid to Third World countries and to underwrite more of the costs of maintaining American military bases in Japan.

The outcome of this reassessment of the U.S.-Japan security relationship was greater Japanese defense spending but not a significant increase in Japan's share of the burden. To show how the new consensus that facilitated these developments was reached, we identify five groups and their perceptions and responses to the U.S.-Japan security relationship. From these five different viewpoints, a mainstream view emerged that merely endorsed the completion of Japan's 1976 defense plan by 1990. Under this plan, Japan will not have any military offensive capability; she will still be protected by America's nuclear shield; and the United States will still enjoy its hegemonic relationship with Japan.

In all democracies, support of the media and the public is crucial for the success of government policies. Our third question asks how the Japanese media perceived Japan's foreign relations with the Soviet Union, the United States, and other Asian countries, and whether public opinion on defense underwent any fundamental change between the 1960s and the 1980s. We find that before the late 1970s powerful newspapers in Japan were critical of U.S. foreign policy and interpreted major events in Asia from a left-of-center point of view. Although one of the top three dailies became slightly supportive of more defense spending in the 1980s and more critical of the Soviet Union's military buildup in Asia, the rest still opposed any change in the status quo for Japan's security relations with the United States.

Meanwhile, public opinion in the 1980s generally supported more defense spending, provided that overall defense spending did not increase abruptly. Although Japanese national pride was piqued by mounting American criticism over the trade issue and the defense "free ride" issue, neither the media nor dominant public opinion has shown any signs of revising the U.S.-Japan security relationship and dramatically altering Japan's defense policies.

In many countries, a defense industry becomes linked to powerful interest groups in the government and to powerful business enterprises eager for lucrative state contracts for military procurement. Our fourth question asks whether Japan's defense industry has become a new force to lobby for more defense spending and whether there are interest groups with ties to the defense industry that could promote a resurgent militarism, as some critics fear.[17] Chapter 5 describes how the military procurement by the Self-Defense Forces actually operates and how military procurement contracts are assigned to manufacturing enterprises. The defense industry is still extremely small and conducts little research and development compared to its counterparts in Western Europe and the United States. The defense industry is also tightly regulated by various state agencies and contributes only a small share of the value-added product of Japanese manufacturing. In fact, the status and management of the defense industry seem to reflect the current public and political consensus for maintaining a modest defense establishment.

Our fifth question asks what kind of defense system Japan has developed in the 1980s. New strategic thinking has defined a role for the Self-Defense Forces and their cooperation with U.S. forces. Chapter 6 describes Japan's defense and military capabilities in the 1980s. The substantive elements of the U.S.-Japan security alliance as formed in 1951 are still intact. The United States is still the mainstay of Japan's defense in the event of regional or world war. Japan upgrades the Self-Defense Forces according to the 1976 Outline, an arms buildup target, and when the 1976 defense plan has been achieved, the Self-Defense Forces will merely provide for a limited defense of Japan and its sea lines of communication for 1,000 nautical miles offshore. The roles of the Self-Defense Forces are basically ambiguous because the only credible threat scenarios are a direct Soviet invasion and a world war, both of which are effectively deterred by the U.S. presence.

This brings us to our sixth and final question: Is there a new military mission Japan can assume that would facilitate a more equal partnership between the two allies to maintain peace in the Pacific Basin and that would do more for Japan's defense? In Chapter 7 we point out that the sea routes connecting the Suez Canal and the Persian Gulf to Japan, and Japan with the United States and the Panama Canal, benefit not only Japan but all Asian states. The economic benefits for Japan and other Asian states that these sea lines of communication provide are considerable, because these states depend so heavily upon seaborne foreign trade.

These Asian sea lines of communication, threatened in recent years by regional wars such as that between Iraq and Iran or the unlikely event of a war with the Soviet Union, have been solely defended by a vast security system created by the United States since World War II. The sum spent each year by the United States for this security system is substantial. Both the United States and Japan now face serious dilemmas. Like the other Asian-Pacific states and territories, Japan needs these sea line of communication to be protected, whereas the United States faces economic difficulties in sustaining its security commitments in the Asian-Pacific region.

In our final chapter, we argue that the present security relationship, whereby Japan spends marginally each year for defense while still remaining heavily dependent on United States defense forces, will not solve these twin dilemmas confronting the two partners. We also argue that if the United States demands more burden-sharing by Japan without granting her more equivalence in power and decision-making to manage security in Asian and the Pacific Basin, then U.S.-Japan relations will become more strained because of threatening trade protectionism within the United States. To prevent further serious deterioration in U.S.-Japan relations, we recommend that both partners reassess their security alliance to facilitate Japan's new role to help the United States protect the sea lines of communication in the Pacific Basin.

We propose a new cooperative agreement based on a NATO-type arrangement to defend the sea lines of communication some 5,000 km from Japan. The United States could transfer to Japan part of its Seventh Fleet and support units for an agreed-upon sum. The two nations could then closely cooperate to provide for the defense of Japan as well as the 5,000 km perimeter around Japan. This new alliance would be a relationship based upon greater equivalence than has existed in the past. Japan's management of its security would be upgraded, and America's burden to provide for the Asian-Pacific security system would be reduced. Far from terminating America's postwar security system in the region, this proposed revision of the two countries' security relationship would still preserve much of it.

While there might be reluctance in Japan to agree to such a reassessment of its security relationship with the United States because of public opinion and different schools of opposing argument, we believe that discussion in Japan would eventually lead to a public endorsement that Japan and the United States develop the new security alliance we propose. A security relationship based upon greater equivalence and mutual responsibility is far superior to a security relationship based upon dependency and growing ill will and deep mistrust. U.S.-Japan security relations are now at an important crossroads.

The present relationship will not be able to survive for very long the new demands that political interest groups in Washington now try to impose. Therefore, a reassessment of the U.S.-Japan security relationship along the argument proposed by this study should be seriously considered.

Notes

1. Paul Kennedy, *The Rise and Fall of the Great Powers* (New York: Random House, 1987).

2. David P. Calleo, *Beyond American Hegemony: The Future of the Western Alliance* (New York: Basic Books, 1987).

3. Samuel P. Huntington, "Coping with the Lippman Gap," *Foreign Affairs*, vol. 66, no. 3 (1988), pp. 453–477.

4. Leonard Silk, "Proposals to Keep the U.S. on Top," *New York Times*, April 1, 1988, p. 28(Y).

5. Staffan Burenstam Linder, *The Pacific Century: Economic and Political Consequences of Asian-Pacific Dynamism* (Stanford, Calif.: Stanford University Press, 1986).

6. Louis Kraar, "The New Powers of Asia," *Fortune*, March 28, 1988, p. 127.

7. "Can Asia's Four Tigers Be Tamed?" *Business Week,* February 15, 1988, p. 46. These figures are not corrected for inflation.

8. Keizai Koho Center, *Japan 1988: An International Comparison* (Tokyo: Japan Institute for Social and Economic Affairs, 1987), p. 40.

9. Ibid., p. 36.

10. Karel G. van Wolferen, "The Japan Problem," *Foreign Affairs,* winter 1986/87, pp. 288–303.

11. "The Tokyo Declaration," *New York Times,* May 4, 1986, p. E-7.

12. Many studies could be cited, but certainly the most recent tough-minded review advanced to lay out a new relationship for the United States and Japan can be found in Edward A. Olsen, *U.S.-Japan Strategic Reciprocity: A New Internationalist View* (Stanford, Calif.: Hoover Institution Press, 1985).

13. Council of Economic Advisers, *Economic Report of the President: Transmitted to the Congress February 1988* (Washington, D.C.: United States Government Printing Office, 1988), pp. 250–251.

14. For a review of this new debate see Peter Schmeisser, "Taking Stock: Is America in Decline?" *New York Times Magazine,* April 17, 1988, pp. 24–28, 64–67 and 96.

15. Tetsuya Kataoka, *The Price of a Constitution: The Origin of Japan's Postwar Politics* (unpublished manuscript).

16. Alvin H. Bernstein, "The Soviets in Cam Ranh Bay," *The National Interest,* spring 1986, p. 19.

17. Examples of such anxiety about a resurgent militarism can be found in Theodore H. White, "The Danger from Japan," *New York Times Magazine,* July 28, 1985; Henry Scott Stokes, "Lost Samurai: The Withered Soul of Postwar Japan," *Harpers,* October 1985, pp. 55–62.

2

The Yoshida Strategy and Its Revision

Japan's defense policy is the reflection of the overall U.S.-Japanese relationship, in which the United States figures as the superordinate power. However, this condition alone does not explain Japan's external conduct, which the Japanese liken to that of medieval Venice, an unarmed merchant state. Beginning with the U.S. occupation, Japan's domestic institutions have been altered and adapted to the nation's external conditions with the support or acquiescence of the Japanese themselves. Japan's external conduct results from the interaction of America's Japan policy with Japan's own domestic politics. It was Prime Minister Shigeru Yoshida who blended the two to produce today's Japan, with all its strengths and weaknesses. Yoshida's foreign policy took form in the 1945-1960 period. In the twenty-eight years that have elapsed since, Japan's foreign policy has undergone substantial changes, which are examined in later chapters.

The Origin of the Yoshida Strategy

We must begin in the early summer of 1945. Berlin had fallen in May amid utter destruction. Japan was doomed. In vain and in ignorance of the Yalta Agreement, the Japanese government was seeking Soviet intercession in the war in the Pacific to save what was left of the empire. Listening in on the Japanese diplomatic traffic, Washington was confirmed in its suspicion that the only thing that stood in the way of Japan's early surrender was its fear for the integrity of the monarchy. If the Allies insisted on unconditional surrender, they would have to carry the war to the mainland. Stalin, who was already violating the Yalta Agreement over Poland, seemed fully capable of winning a concession from Japan at the expense of the United States. Washington's counsel was divided about retreating from unconditional surrender, but President Roosevelt's death seemed to tip the scale in favor of accepting a conditional surrender.

Henry Stimson, secretary of the army, and Joseph C. Grew, former ambassador to Tokyo who was then acting secretary of state while Secretary Stettinius busied himself with the United Nations, held the sway. Unless the Allies saved and used the Emperor, they argued, disarmament and occupation of Japan would be impossible. And they succeeded in drafting an ultimatum, to be issued from the Potsdam conference of Allied leaders in July, intended to signify that the surrender expected of Japan was less than unconditional. Upon receiving the Potsdam Declaration, officials in Japan, too, were split. The Foreign Ministry and the peace faction understood the drafters' intention and recommended surrender forthwith on that basis. Yoshida, son-in-law of a former Privy Seal and imperial adviser, belonged to both groups. But the Imperial Army demanded a confirmation expressly guaranteeing the integrity of imperial prerogatives. Another exchange of notes took place between Tokyo and Washington before Japan surrendered amid the destruction of Hiroshima and Nagasaki.

In August, however, the Truman administration carried out a major reshuffling of cabinet posts. James Byrnes replaced Stettinius as secretary of state, and Stimson retired from Army. Grew also retired, and Byrnes appointed Dean Acheson undersecretary of state. With that, the State Department became distinctly hostile to the idea of sparing the Emperor and the monarchical institution. Washington's first major policy guideline to General Douglas MacArthur, Supreme Commander of Allied Powers (SCAP), was a ringing manifesto of New Deal zeal that envisioned something like a French Revolution, to be carried out through the "freely expressed will of the Japanese people."[1]

On the basis of the Potsdam Declaration, Japan's surrender was unconditional, the United States insisted. Legally speaking, there was nothing improper about this construction of the declaration. However, the Japanese government was duty-bound to disagree. Writing to Truman in October 1945, MacArthur noted "the extraordinarily dangerous and inherently inflammable situation which exists here."[2] When MacArthur was ordered to proceed with constitutional revision as part of occupation reforms, the safety of the Emperor and the throne was placed on the line. Prime Minister Kijurō Shidehara and his foreign minister, Yoshida, made desperate efforts to stave off constitutional revision and to prevail with their construction of the Potsdam Declaration.

It was MacArthur who saved the Emperor and averted disastrous consequences. A conservative Republican with presidential ambitions, he was inclined to be critical of the Roosevelt administration's conduct of war. Even before he set foot in Japan, he was already determined to save the Emperor. "The preservation of the Emperor system was my fixed purpose," MacArthur later said. "It was inherent and integral to the Japanese political and cultural survival.

The vicious efforts to destroy the person of the Emperor and thereby abolish the system became one of the most dangerous menaces that threatened the successful rehabilitation of the nation."[3]

To preempt any attempt on the Emperor, MacArthur drafted a constitution expressly upholding the monarchy but transferring sovereignty to the people, and he urged the Japanese government to adopt it forthwith. Acceptance of the war-renouncing Article IX was the condition for the Emperor's safety. With great reluctance, Japanese officials acceded to MacArthur. As far as they were concerned, the constitution was a substitute for the Potsdam Declaration and a contract to save the Emperor. To them, this was the sole significance of the constitution. Yoshida did not accept it because it was democratic or for its own sake, as many have alleged since. It was for this reason that Yoshida would later use the constitution as a tool of his policy, giving the Americans a taste of their own medicine.

Besides the constitution, one other aspect of occupation reform would later profoundly affect Japan's foreign relations and domestic politics. In the initial, New Deal phase of the occupation, a phase in which U.S.-Soviet cooperation was the norm, MacArthur sought to drastically alter Japan's political landscape through an extensive purge of existing political forces on the one hand and the unleashing of the left wing on the other. The communists were liberated from jail with the expectation that they would spearhead the revolution. The Japan Socialist Party (JSP) was also founded with the blessing of MacArthur, who hoped the Socialists, led by a Christian, would become the center and mainstay of Japan. When they emerged as the party of plurality in the 1947 election, they were encouraged to organize a coalition government.

While the radical, early reforms—the constitution, land reform, the establishment of the left—were underway, the United States in 1948 executed a major policy reversal because of the Cold War. It was a stunning change, symbolized by the often-bandied-about phrase "We fought the wrong enemy." Under George F. Kennan's direction from the State Department, the New Deal-type reforms were superseded by a new program designed to rehabilitate Japan as a potential ally in the containment policy. Ultimately, after the Korean War, the reversal was to culminate in the conclusion of a treaty of alliance with Japan.

This meant that the United States had two sets of occupation policies in Japan, policies based on mutually contradictory assumptions about Japan and the world. The capstone of the early policies was the constitution, and the later policies culminated in the 1951 U.S.-Japan security treaty. The constitution was eagerly defended by its beneficiary, the Socialists, and their existence in turn was protected by it. The anti-communist military alliance was equally eagerly endorsed by the conservatives. Most of Japan's subsequent problems in foreign and domestic policies can be traced directly to the tension between the legacies of early and later occupation policies. The only rational solution to the problem was to revise the constitution to make it compatible with the military alliance. (The JSP's attempt to abolish the military alliance on the grounds of its unconstitutionality was self-destructive.) As we shall see, the United States and the Japanese conservatives would try to change the constitution—but in vain.

When a peace treaty with Japan was placed on the agenda in 1949–1950, three major contenders emerged. The Joint Chiefs of Staff (JCS) and the Defense Department demanded "de facto peace," whereby the United States would keep virtually all of occupation power and privileges intact but would give the Japanese domestic autonomy. John Foster Dulles, a Republican placed in charge of negotiating the treaty for the Democratic administration in the spirit of bipartisanship, wanted an anti-communist ally in Japan. Thus, he insisted on formal equality for Japan. He agreed with the JCS on the need for constitutional revision and rearmament, but he collided with the JCS' desire for continued occupation.

A third party consisted of MacArthur and Yoshida. Yoshida's conservative party had just won a resounding victory and a comfortable majority at the expense of the Socialists in the 1949 election, and he had established himself as a Cold War ally of America. Yoshida was his own man and played cat and mouse with MacArthur. But he also knew that Japan's fortune in treaty negotiations was utterly dependent on MacArthur, who exercised inordinate influence in Washington for a military commander. Yoshida apparently decided that it was wise for Japan to scrupulously observe MacArthur's proclivities.

MacArthur's vision of Japan can be summed up as Philippinization. The inspiration for his no-war constitution apparently came from the no-war constitution of that American colony. Just as the presence of the Subic Bay and Clark bases obviated the need for anything more than constabulary forces in the Philippines, so, MacArthur assumed, Japan could dispense with its own armed forces if the United States kept its presence in Okinawa but not in Japan proper. He held fast to this belief even after the Korean War took him by surprise, and he collided with Dulles and the JCS. At the root of MacArthur's insistence on the Philippinized Japan was his extraordinary attachment to the constitution he had laid down. In several tense exchanges with the Pentagon brass, he asserted that the prestige of the United States would be tarnished if it were to reverse itself over so basic a reform.

The final form of peace with Japan consisted of two treaties in one package—the peace and security treaties, representing respectively the bureaucratic interests of the State and Defense departments. The State Department won the peace treaty based on formal equality for Japan, and the Defense Department won de facto occupation. The contradiction between the two was papered over with a device whereby Japan—made "independent" with the conclusion of the peace treaty—would volunteer to accept an indefinite U.S. presence.

Dulles was charged with the difficult task of maintaining bipartisan foreign policy and negotiating the two treaties through the Senate, where the Republicans dwelt on the "sellout" at Yalta and the "loss of China" to obstruct the Democratic administration. Dulles was aware that if MacArthur—a favorite dark-horse presidential candidate for the Republicans—so much as criticized the treaties, the chances for Senate ratification were nil. "General MacArthur," Dulles said, "must be one hundred percent behind the treaty."[4] Dulles agreed to retain the constitution in exchange for the general's endorsement of the treaties.[5] Through this second MacArthur intervention, the no-war constitution—the very antithesis of war—was superimposed on the treaty of military alliance.

MacArthur justified the Philippinized Japan on two grounds: that Japan could not afford rearmament, and that a rearmed Japan would threaten its neighbors. The latter thesis is still being invoked by both the Japanese and the U.S. governments today to justify the small-Japan alternative.

But the differences between MacArthur, Dulles, and the Pentagon should not be unduly exaggerated. Dulles described the U.S.-Japanese tie based on the two treaties as "the relationship of mutual security . . . under which presumably the military power would be so apportioned that Japan could not itself be an *offensive military threat* and the relationship between the victor and vanquished would be so intimate and integrated as to *make incredible a war of revenge.*"[6] That is, the treaties served the dual purpose of defending Japan against communist menace and of defending the United States against Japan. The rearmament the Pentagon demanded was essentially for defensive purposes. And Dulles's notion of equality was purely formal.

MacArthur's second intervention on behalf of his constitution produced a mixed result. On the one hand, he helped Dulles tone down some of the Pentagon's demands he regarded as "imperialistic." On the other hand, he encouraged Yoshida's resistance to rearmament, the condition of mutual security and Japan's formal equality. Rebuffed by Yoshida, Dulles snubbed him with an obviously unequal treaty, which, for example, authorized U.S. military intervention in the event of domestic disorders in Japan. Yoshida thus became vulnerable to the charges of his political enemies that by refusing military self-help he had sold out Japan's sovereignty.

Yoshida was hard-nosed about the security treaty. He was sure that leasing bases with most of the occupation privilege intact was a fair price for U.S. protection. He did not feel called upon to contribute to self-help, because Washington was insisting on keeping an indefinite "regime of control" anyway. No wording of the treaty, he assured his critics, could alter the fact of Japan's weakness as a vanquished power. Rather, Japan should turn the predicament to its advantage by concentrating on economic recovery. That would hasten the coming of the day when Japan could claim real equality and become a real ally of America. He was quoted by a bemused American official as saying, "When it is objected that Japan will become a colony of the United States, [I] always repl[y] that, just as the United States was once a colony of the Great Britain but now is the stronger of the two, if Japan became a colony of the United States, it will also eventually become the stronger."[7]

Much touted as a herald of equality and independence, the San Francisco Peace Treaty created a temporary euphoria in Japan, after nearly seven years of military rule. But that euphoria soon dissipated, as the Japanese discovered the reality of the U.S. presence. The Cold War was at its height, and the East-West tension was reproduced in the domestic political alignment. The JSP—previously MacArthur's centrist party—became radicalized by the increasingly powerful left wing. And the left wing has defined the party's characteristic ever since: neutralism; peace with all the belligerents, including the Soviet Union and China rather than with the West alone; opposition to U.S. bases; and opposition to rearmament.

The security treaty also created a new alignment among the conservatives. The conservative politicians who had been banished from public life during the occupation purge came back en masse as a new political force. Let us call them the revisionists. Led by Ichirō Hatoyama and Nobusuke Kishi and supported by such young men as Yasuhiro Nakasone, the revisionists criticized the unequal treaty, Yoshida's alleged "subservience" to Washington, his claim that the Police Reserve forces—created by MacArthur on the morrow of the Korean War—were not an army, and above all his use of the constitution in hitching a free ride on America. Thus, revisions of the constitution and the security treaty and rearmament became the platform of the revisionists. In addition, the revisionists were interested in Japan's diplomatic autonomy and demanded peace treaties with Moscow and Peking.

Of the three foreign policy alternatives in Japan—represented respectively by the Socialists, the Yoshida faction, and the revisionists—the last two have been, and still are, the only viable ones. Note that both Yoshida and the revisionists were nationalists, the only difference being in their policies. In the three-way alignment in politics that appeared after the San Francisco peace conference, different combinations were possible. Only when two groups coalesced could they have their way. On the constitution issue, Yoshida and the Socialists banded together to defend the status quo. On the security treaty, Yoshida's status quo was opposed by the revisionists and the Socialists. On rapprochement with the communist powers, the revisionists and the Socialists were opposed by the Yoshida faction. The three groups were in rough equilibrium and seemed to mutually veto any radical departure.

What broke the logjam was John Foster Dulles's reentry into Japanese politics. Already, the Truman administration had launched the policy designated NSC 68 that was to turn the United States into what Daniel Yergin called the "national security state" with an enormous peacetime standing army and forward deployment of troops in NATO countries and Japan. President Eisenhower, who took office in 1953, appointed Dulles secretary of state and carried that policy forward to a new height by concluding additional alliances on the periphery of the Soviet Union. Dulles decided that rearmament of Japan, frustrated by MacArthur and Yoshida, must be completed once and for all. He enlisted the revisionists, led by Hatoyama, as his ally for the task and began to exert pressure on Yoshida. Vice-President Richard Nixon was dispatched to Tokyo in 1955, and in an attempt to smoke Yoshida out of his constitutional lair, he publicly admitted that the MacArthur constitution was a "mistake."

Dulles offered economic and military assistance under the Mutual Security Assistance Act to help Japan rearm. Yoshida fought back as best he could. He had to rely on the Socialists, who defended the constitution as his proxy.[8] But he became so isolated in 1954 that he succumbed partially to Dulles: he agreed to a bill authorizing the establishment of the Self-Defense Forces, with 220,000 men in three services. The Self-Defense Forces, Yoshida averred, were in lieu of army, navy, and air force, which were still unconstitutional. Thus, Yoshida initiated the distinction between reality (*hon'ne*) and facade (*tatemae*). The Socialists were holding fast to the constitutional facade, while the conservatives supported the reality of military alliance and rearmament by the back door.

But we must view this event in perspective: Yoshida relented on the need for self-help. With that, the difference between Dulles and Yoshida narrowed. Dulles demanded a military force of 350,000, roughly equal to the peacetime standing force of the Imperial Army in the 1920s. He justified it with the assumption that a Soviet invasion of Japan on the order of the Korean War was likely. Yoshida held fast to MacArthur's assumption that discounted such a scenario, and he has been proved correct. From here on, the difference between Dulles and Yoshida was not over self-help vs. free ride but over how much self-help was adequate for Japan.

Between Secretary Dulles's attempt to eliminate the MacArthur legacy in Japan with the help of the revisionists and Yoshida's attempt to resist him with the help of the Socialists, Japan's politics were radicalized in the years between the San Francisco conference and 1955. In election after election, the Socialists expanded with alarming speed on the platform of anti-American neutralism. As Table 2.1 indicates, the left wing, which split the party over the peace and security treaty issue in 1951, was expanding faster; by the time the party reunited in 1955, the whole party was under the left's domination.

Japan in the second half of the 1950s was standing at a crossroads. The issues were rearmament and what kind of relationship with America was desirable. From 1947 to 1948, before the Cold War intensified, non-alignment was postulated while George F. Kennan was the controlling voice at the State Department. But that was a closed issue after San Francisco. By then, there were only two realistic choices. One was the Adenauer model, proposed by Dulles and

TABLE 2.1
ELECTION RESULTS IN THE LOWER HOUSE (1946-1958)
(by number of seats)

Year	Conservative Parties	JSP Left	JSP Right	JCP*	Others
1946	272	94		5	129
1947	291	143		4	34
1949	333	48		35	50
1952	325	54	57	0	30
1953	310	72	66	1	17
1955	297	89	67	2	12
1958	287	166		1	13

* Japan Communist Party

Source: Seizaburō Satō and Tetsuhisa Matsuzaki, *Jimintō
seiken* [The Liberal Democratic Party Regime]
(Tokyo: Chūō Kōronsha, 1986), pp. 356-359.

endorsed by the revisionists. Had Yoshida been persuaded to abandon the
MacArthur legacy and follow this road, he and the revisionists together would
have enjoyed an overwhelming majority with which to outvote the Socialists on
all issues. Under the circumstances, the JSP was likely to have taken the course
chosen by the German Social Democratic Party in the 1959 congress in Bad
Godesburg, which endorsed moderate social democracy for platform. It was this
choice that paved the way for the emergence of pro-NATO socialist chancellors
like Willy Brandt and Helmut Schmidt.[9]

But Yoshida had already paid too much for the constitution, was caught up in
the heat of partisan battle with Hatoyama, and refused to stand down—unless
forced. He was reported to have said:

> We can never pull off the so-called rearmament for the time being, nor is
> there any interest in it among the people. On the other hand, it is not
> something that justifies the government's initiative to impose on them.
> The day [we rearm] will come naturally if the livelihood recovers. It may
> sound selfish, but let the Americans handle [our security] until then. It is
> indeed our God-given luck that the Constitution bans arms. If the Americans
> complain, the constitution gives us an adequate cover. The politicians who
> want to amend it are oafs.[10]

Yoshida's alternative was to pit the Socialists (pro-constitution) against the
revisionists (pro-alliance) to keep both the constitution and the alliance. It is in

this context that we must see the surge of the JSP in the late 1950s. Ideally, Yoshida needed the JSP to be just strong enough to block constitutional amendment—which requires a two-thirds vote of the two houses—but not so strong as to threaten the conservative rule or the American connection.

But the Socialists were growing stronger and began to boast of taking power peacefully in a few more elections. In late 1954, they joined hands with Hatoyama to bring down the Yoshida government. Then they unified the two wings in a merger in 1955. This was a grave threat to the conservatives. To cope with it, the Hatoyama faction took the lead in unifying all the conservatives into a single party, named the Liberal Democratic Party (LDP), a few months later. This was the beginning of the so-called 1955 system of left-right division. The LDP at its founding was an anti-Yoshida party of the revisionists. Hatoyama was now prime minister and vowed to do the "opposite of everything" Yoshida had done.

Unfortunately, he chose the peace treaty with the Soviet Union as his first act in office and ran into Washington's objection. Hatoyama wanted the treaty to match Yoshida's, concluded in San Francisco. "Autonomy" appeared frequently in his rhetoric, but, being a strong anti-communist, he most certainly did not intend to undermine the American connection. Besides, disarmed and helpless, Japan in the mid-1950s simply lacked the wherewithal to chart an independent course. Hatoyama probably had in mind something like Willy Brandt's latter-day Ostpolitik, involving a formal tie with Moscow and a territorial settlement. On the other hand, the Japanese Socialists warmly endorsed Hatoyama's Ostpolitik, ushering in the first and only period of bipartisanship in postwar foreign policy. Furthermore, Nikita Khrushchev, who had emerged as Stalin's successor, wanted an opening to Japan as part of his "thaw." These moves appeared to cause Dulles to suspect that Hatoyama might pave the way toward rampant neutralism. Earlier, in San Francisco, Dulles had objected to Japan's peace treaty with the People's Republic of China and forced Yoshida to conclude one with the Chinese Nationalist government instead. Dulles's idea of military alliance presupposed something akin to a state of war, precluding political relations with the "enemy." In this he was too truculent, and he would pay a price.

The treaty negotiations between Japan and the Soviet Union focused on the settlement of the Northern Territories, the four islands off Hokkaido occupied by Soviet forces since 1945. Moscow offered two of them back as the final settlement, and Hatoyama agreed. But Secretary Dulles intervened to thwart the settlement by arguing that Japan should claim all four islands. He maintained that if Japan were to cede two islands to the Soviet Union, the United States was entitled to claim Okinawa and the Bonin Islands in turn. He rested his case on an article in the peace treaty by which Japan promised equal concessions to all allied powers. Yoshida supported Dulles, probably out of enmity for

Hatoyama and in order to reverse his fortune. The Dulles demarche proved conclusive, and no peace treaty has been signed to this day.[11]

The revisionists suffered a setback, but Hatoyama was not finished yet. His last hurrah was the so-called small district bill to replace the existing multimember electoral district with a single-member, winner-take-all system. Accompanied by large-scale gerrymandering, the bill was designed to reduce the Socialist strength below one-third of the Diet, so as to carry out the constitutional revision. But once again Yoshida outsmarted the revisionists. This time, his united front with the Socialists successfully pigeonholed the bill. Hatayama sustained his "biggest loss" and retired.[12]

The death of the small district bill in 1956 ratified the permanence of the constitution and the Socialists. At the same time, however, the JSP's electoral fortunes began to stagnate in the elections of 1955–56: the JSP could block constitutional revision but was otherwise impotent. These events came on top of the Dulles maneuver that completed the protectorate arrangement for Japan, cutting it off from Moscow and Peking in a world in which the East-West axis constituted the stuff of world politics. Dulles still wanted rearmament, but the revisionists began to lose interest in it. The fact of the matter was that the LDP no longer faced any threat: internally it was supreme and externally it was secure.

It was the convergence of all these critical events in late 1956 that produced another change in Japanese politics—the LDP broke up into eight or nine factions, depending on how one counted, each with a formal organization or the trappings of an independent party. The LDP could afford the luxury because it now had a permanent tenure in power. Change in power could take place only within the LDP's factions, much as in the Democratic primaries in the one-party American South. With this development, Japan's postwar political system was fully articulated. In this system, the collusion of the Yoshida faction with the Socialists would foster the withdrawal syndrome in foreign policy and Allied military cooperation, while factionalism in the ruling party would result in low articulation of the national will.[13]

But the revisionists would mount a final counterattack, led by Prime Minister Nobusuke Kishi, who took on the security treaty revision against all odds. To overcome Yoshida's objection to treaty revision, Kishi had to enlist the uncertain help of the Socialists, who were also opposed to the unequal treaty. Unfortunately for Kishi, the Socialists began to have second thoughts about tighter military integration of Japan with the United States following the Soviet launching of Sputnik (1957) and the Quemoy crisis in the Taiwan Strait (1958). In a reversal, the JSP decided to oppose treaty revision, that is, to defend the status quo on the treaty while keeping up the rhetoric of opposing it. With the Socialists and Yoshida both opposed to treaty revision, Kishi was completely isolated and vulnerable. He leaned on Eisenhower and Dulles, who stood by him and offered to visit him in Tokyo to boost his cause. But that undermined him instead, for he looked more and more like the "running dog" of "American imperialism" that the radicals said he was. The JSP and the Communists mounted monumental and violent demonstrations to oppose President Eisenhower's visit to Tokyo, finally forcing Kishi to cancel it. Yoshida waited until Kishi was sufficiently weakened before he went to Kishi's rescue on one condition: Kishi was to resign after the passage of the treaty in favor of Yoshida's own follower, Ikeda. Kishi was sacrificed for the passage of the treaty and Yoshida's victory.

Kishi's downfall concluded an era, in which the Japanese took initiative to improve their status in foreign relations, a fact that is hard to imagine from today's perspective. From here on, the Japanese government was headed by a succession of prime ministers tutored in the so-called Yoshida School. The Socialists and the conservative revisionists remained on the scene, but they stopped challenging the security treaty and the constitution.

Even though the safe passage of the security treaty in the face of Socialist opposition was a credit to the conservative LDP, Ikeda played it down. He distanced himself from the military alliance, security affairs, and foreign relations in general. Those were, he indicated, political risks. Instead, he unveiled a platform that captivated the Japanese for more than a decade thereafter: the national income-doubling plan. Ikeda spoke of "patience and tolerance" for the Socialist opposition, and he began to cultivate a special relationship with the JSP once he was in power. He quietly assured them that the LDP would follow a species of conservative pacifist policies. A succession of policy pronouncements followed: the Three Principles of Nuclear Disarmament declared that Japan would not possess, manufacture, or introduce nuclear weapons (with obvious impact on the freedom of U.S. military movements in and about Japan); weapons export, which fueled Japan's recovery during the Korean War, was now banned twice over by Diet resolutions; commemorating Hiroshima and Nagasaki became a national exercise; the government vowed that it would take a "political low profile" and "separate politics from economics"; and finally, the government declared it would not spend more than 1 percent of GNP on defense.

Beside the constitutional status quo, this amounted to a huge concession, indeed a capitulation, to the Socialists. And here the 1955 system of left-right division went through the final transformation. Under Hatoyama and Kishi, the division was an outright confrontation, across what was called the "domestic 38th Parallel." Now the division was based on subtle collusion, which the Japanese euphemistically called "consensus." The JSP had switched to de facto support of the treaty during the Quemoy crisis (by opposing treaty revision). Nonetheless, it kept up formal opposition to the alliance in inflammatory rhetoric. And the LDP chose to respect the Socialists' hypersensitivity on security issues.

Though divisive political issues seldom came up any more, there were bills and votes that the Socialists regarded as critical. In a straight partisan vote, the LDP majority could never lose. However, with the backing of the media, the JSP would demand the rule of unanimity (that is, "consensus") by castigating the majority principle as the "violence of numbers." To have their way without alienating the Socialists, the LDP's floor managers in the Diet would enter into horse-trading and bargaining. This usually took place in the Diet Management Committee, a counterpart of the House of Representatives' Ways and Means Committee, which acted as the traffic cop over parliamentary agenda. Somehow, Socialist support for a "consensus" would be procured and the Diet restored to normalcy.[14]

The effect of all this was profound. Externally, the JSP, holding fast to the constitution and anti-Americanism, provided a screen for the conservatives. Washington, hostage to fear of communism, concluded from the riots of 1960 that Japan had to be left alone with its domestic priorities. The U.S. strategic superiority was still unchallenged, and the American presence, though dwindling, was quite sufficient to deter aggression. U.S.-Japanese relations became synonymous with trade relations.

The impact of the 1955 system was most pronounced on the Socialists, who began to live a life of contradiction—keeping up anti-nuclear demonstrations and laying siege to the American bases while their very pacifist existence was guaranteed by the Pax Americana. Domestically, they kept up their revolutionary rhetoric and class orientation. Still, they could maintain their existence because of support provided by the Sōhyō federations of labor unions, another legacy of the occupation reforms. But as the 1960s wore on and the Japanese standard of living shot up, union members lost their ardor and slowly but steadily slipped out of the Socialist ranks. The JSP kept sliding down as competing opposition parties drew away its constituency.

A Summing Up

What can we conclude from the foregoing analysis of Japan's postwar politics up to 1975, when the latest change was introduced?

(1) The no-war constitution was a necessity for U.S.-Japanese friendship, rather than the product of MacArthur's whim or inclination to coddle the Japanese. It was MacArthur's second intervention that had to be questioned.

(2) The Japanese were not always as passive politically as they are today. Until 1960, they actively sought to improve their status by rearming.

(3) Though the contradiction in occupation policy was beyond Japan's control, it did have a good chance to discard the MacArthur legacy and develop along the Adenauer model. Ironically, it was Dulles's collaboration with Yoshida that thwarted that development. John Foster Dulles could not live with

Yoshida, nor could he live with Hatoyama. In the final analysis, America and Japan were victims of mutual distrust born of World War II.

(4) Did Japan's defense get a "free ride" from the United States? We have to be precise about what we mean by that. The difference between what Japan would have had to pay if she were autonomous (in the sense that Britain and France are autonomous in the Atlantic alliance) and what she has actually paid is large, and this difference was a saving to Japan and a burden on the United States. But the U.S. military protection of Japan was designed to forestall such autonomy. Within the framework of U.S. protection, Japan has not been forthcoming on self-defense either. But the difference between what Washington demanded and Japan's actual contribution has been a difference in degree, not in kind. The difference is between 350,000 men and 220,000 men in arms, or an armed force we might call the Adenauer model and Adenauer minus. Japan has enjoyed not a free ride, but a cheap ride.

(5) Granted that a cheap ride was a saving to Japan, was Japan's economic development helped by that cheap ride? That is, was the cost difference between the Adenauer model and Adenauer minus such as to materially aid Japan's development? The answer is negative. It seems highly unlikely that Japan's development could have been hindered by marginally increasing its defense burden to a par with, say, West Germany. In the cases of the Federal Republic of Germany, the Republic of Korea, and the Republic of China, heavy rearmament was not a hindrance to economic development. We must remember that Japan's high-speed growth of 10 percent-plus in GNP terms started in 1955 under Hatoyama, long before Yoshida's victory in 1960. Had Hatoyama won, Japan would have terminated the cheap ride and produced the "economic miracle."

On the other hand, military dependence entails psychological cost, which is intangible but real. Paradoxically, the Japanese—with Yoshida's guidance—turned that psychological cost of dependence to good account. When the Japanese realized that they had to resign themselves to their status under the security treaty of 1960, they resolved to compensate for their status with economic achievement. Max Weber, the German sociologist and the most authoritative thinker on capitalist development, put it as follows:

> National or religious minorities which are in a position of subordination to a group of rulers are likely, through their voluntary or involuntary exclusion from positions of political influence, to be driven with peculiar force into economic activity. Their ablest members seek to satisfy the desire for recognition of their abilities in this field, since there is no opportunity in the service of the State.[15]

(6) The constitution was originally accepted as merely an expediency. But after Yoshida's victory in 1960, the LDP became pacifistic, and the constitution

became to a degree an end in itself. Legitimizing the LDP's power and its phenomenal growthmanship policy, the constitution commanded respect, as any other stable constitution does. In time, other institutions—factionalism, the "consensus" myth, and so on—coalesced around the constitution. In this way, the Japanese undergirded it with a network of personalized relationships that constitute the essence of a Japanese organization. Once the extra-constitutional support for the constitution had grown, the Japanese were in a sense ensnared by it.

Much to Yoshida's chagrin, the constitution was already striking roots while he was still alive. Shortly before his death in 1964, he said of his earlier objection to rearmament, "But that was when I was serving in the cabinet. In view of subsequent developments, I have come to have many doubts over the reality of Japan's defense." He went on to say that during his latest travels through Europe, he had had a chance to observe the leaders of the free world in their efforts to "contribute to the peace and prosperity of the world as their own responsibility." He was "moved" by the sight and "came to feel that Japan, too, ought to make [a similar] contribution. . . ." Furthermore, in an obvious reference to the Ikeda government's way of using the constitution, he said, "As for the Constitution's *tatemae* and the government's policy, I am not one to evade my own share of responsibility. As an official in charge of the constitutional debate and of subsequent administration of the government, I am painfully aware of my responsibility for it."[16]

(7) The constitution acquired a new lease on life when it was wedded to the unequal security treaty. The two go hand in hand. In fact, the constitution may be viewed as a de facto addendum to the treaty affecting the rights and obligations of the parties to it. According to the Japanese government, the constitution does not deny Japan the right of self-defense, which includes the right to solicit and receive Allied military assistance however and wherever it may be necessary. But the constitution prohibits Japan's military cooperation with Allied military forces unless those forces are involved directly in Japan's own defense. It confines Japan's own military actions "to the geographic scope of the Japanese territorial land, sea, and airspace."[17] Japan refuses to project its power beyond this space either singly or jointly. This strategy of so-called passive defense is the foundation of Japan's defense policy. It may be stated as a proposition that as long as the security treaty framework is maintained, Japan will have no incentive to change the policy.

Notes

1. "United States Initial Postsurrender Policy for Japan" (SWNCC 150/4), cited in John M. Maki (ed.), *Conflict and Tension in the Far East: Key Documents, 1894–1960* (Seattle: University of Washington Press, 1961), pp. 124–132.

2. D. Clayton James, *The Years of MacArthur. III: Triumph and Disaster, 1945–1964* (New York: Houghton Mifflin, 1985), p. 22.

3. Ibid., p. 129.

4. U.S. Department of State, *Foreign Relations of the United States, 1951* (Washington, D.C.: Government Printing Office, 1980), VI, Pt. 1, pp. 822–823.

5. See Tetsuya Kataoka, *The Price of a Constitution: The Origin of Japan's Postwar Politics* (unpublished manuscript), Chapter 3, for further documentation.

6. Memorandum of conversation by Dulles, Paris, June 1951, U.S. Department of State, *Foreign Relations of the United States, 1951,* VI, 1115.

7. U.S. Department of State, *Foreign Relations of the United States, 1950,* VII, 1166.

8. Tetsuya Kataoka, *The Price of a Constitution,* Chapter 4.

9. See Hideo Ōtake, *Adenauaa to Yoshida Shigeru* [Adenauer and Shigeru Yoshida] (Tokyo: Chūō Kōronsha, 1986).

10. Kiichi Miyazawa, *Tokyo-Washinton no mitsudan* [Secret Talks Between Tokyo and Washington] (Tokyo: Jitsugyō no Nihonsha, 1956), p. 160.

11. See Tetsuya Kataoka, *The Price of a Constitution,* Chapter 5.

12. Ibid.

13. Karel van Wolferen, "The Japan Problem," *Foreign Affairs,* winter 1986/87, argues that there is no "top" in the Japanese government.

14. Apologists for the Yoshida School argue that consensus-type decision-making is a cultural legacy of Japan from time immemorial. Murakami *et al., Bunmei to shite no ie shakai* [The Ie-Society as a Civilization] (Tokyo: Chūō Kōronsha, 1985). We do not challenge the veracity of Murakami's history, but merely suggest that when there are two parallel explanations, the simpler, more straightforward one carries more weight.

15. *The Protestant Ethic and the Spirit of Capitalism* (New York: Unwin Books, 1958), p. 39.

16. Shigeru Yoshida, *Sekai to Nihon* [The World and Japan] (Tokyo: Banchō Shōbō, 1963), pp. 202, 206.

17. Defense Agency, *Defense of Japan, 1987* (Tokyo: The Japan Times, 1987), p. 71. We must note, however, that West Germany operates under similar restraints embodied not in its constitution but elsewhere.

3

The National Debate
over Security

As we have already stated, in the early postwar years Japan's leaders adopted the strategy of allying with the United States and building only a small Self-Defense Force. But after 1975 many Japanese began perceiving that the balance of power in Asia had started to change. Some expressed fear that America's withdrawal from Asia and its economic decline now left in the Pacific Basin a power vacuum that was rapidly being filled by the growing military power of the Soviet Union. Therefore, the question was raised whether Japan's level of defense spending and the size and quality of its Self-Defense Forces were sufficient to maintain the country's defense under the current U.S.-Japan security treaty.

A new debate over Japan's security began to evolve in which a bewildering variety of viewpoints were expressed in leading journals, newspapers, and monographs. To make sense out of these discussions, we have identified five groups that shared some common orientations about the new threat to Japan's national security and about how the government should respond to that threat. The three elements making up these common orientations are the perceived threats to Japan's security, the basic strategy to deal with those threats, and the policies for implementing that strategy. We call our five groups the realists, the diplomats, the conservatives, the nuclear advocates, and the strategists. These people were government officials, military experts, strategists, policy analysts, and journalists. We will argue that these five groups really endorsed only three major options for improving Japan's defense. After 1985, the debate virtually ended, and two of these options were merged to shape the policies that the government now endorses for Japan's defense.

The Realists

The realists perceive that the military balance between the United States and the Soviet Union had shifted in favor of the Soviet Union by the late seventies and that Japan's security became threatened by greater Soviet military power in the Far East. Therefore, Japan must strengthen the U.S.-Japan alliance to help restore a new balance of military power. That can be done only by strengthening the Japanese Self-Defense Forces.

As early as the spring of 1978, Osamu Kaihara, chief of the secretariat of the National Defense Council, shocked many by publicly stating that the Self-Defense Forces "absolutely could not last even 24 hours," because the enemy would destroy the fixed radar sites and air bases at Chitose and Misawa in a single strike.[1] In September 1980, a defense analyst, Takio Yamazaki, noted that there was no central operational command to coordinate the three armed services, and he pointed out that the Self-Defense Forces could not function as a real defense power: twenty-eight radar sites were exposed to air attack; ammunition stockpiles were inadequate; naval torpedoes lacked explosive charges; military training was still inadequate.[2] Moreover, the public had not yet been sufficiently educated to understand why it was so important for Japan to have an effective, modern defense force. Many security experts agreed with these assessments of the Self-Defense Forces' poor capabilities, and others alluded to problems of coordination between the U.S. and Japanese military forces when conducting joint maneuvers and of the low morale on both sides.[3]

In late 1985, a security expert named Hiroyuki Maruyama described in considerable detail the buildup of the Soviet Pacific fleet over the preceding fifteen years. He stressed that the U.S. Seventh Fleet, weakened by having units dispatched to the Persian Gulf, could offer only "sea denial rather than sea control over the three straits" around Japan.[4] In fact, the Soviets' ability to project naval power into the Southwest Pacific had created a new threat to Japan, because Soviet naval forces could now disrupt the sea lanes so vital to Japan's economy. Maruyama's warning echoed the new concerns about the Soviet military expansion.

Yamazaki had pointed out as early as 1980 that, because U.S. Pacific power had been greatly reduced by the shift of units to the Persian Gulf, Soviet naval power was already sufficient to blockade Japan.[5] Such developments facilitated "the Soviet policy of Finlandizing Japan."[6] In that same year, a foreign affairs analyst named Osamu Miyoshi argued that under the detente of the seventies the balance of power had tipped in favor of the Soviet Union.[7] In 1981, the director of the Japanese Defense Agency, Jōji Omura, also stated that the balance of power had shifted in favor of the Soviet Union and that Japan was now severely threatened by the recent Soviet deployment of one-fourth of its ground and air forces and one-third of its naval power to the Far East as well as by the greatly expanded nuclear arsenal in Siberia.[8] Other analysts expressed these same fears.

This accelerating buildup of Soviet military power in the Far East also posed a new threat to Japan in terms of a possible conventional military assault from the north. In early 1979, the defense analyst Hideaki Kase had pointed out that such an attack by conventional military means could come only from the north and that northern Hokkaido was truly Japan's front line of defense.[9] More recently, a Ground Self-Defense Force officer named Shigeki Nishimura argued in November 1985 that Hokkaido, like Sweden and Norway, probably fell within the inner defense perimeter of the Soviet Union and that in an emergency the Soviet Union would consider neutralizing these areas a top priority.[10]

But it was going to be very difficult for Japan to do its share in the alliance if the Self-Defense Forces did not measure up as a modern military force. Developing a more modern military was a critical element for the strategy of the realists. They all shared the basic perspective that the Self-Defense Forces, as of the late seventies and early eighties, suffered major defects that ruled them out as a military force capable of defending Japan—least of all of assisting the United States in providing air and sea surveillance within a 1,000-nautical-mile perimeter around Japan.

Those who shared the realist position on security would probably agree that Japan's Self-Defense Forces should serve as a scarecrow to ward off the birds that threaten to make off with the harvest. Defense Agency director Kōichi Katō recently used this metaphor:

It is correct that scarecrows chase away sparrows just by standing there. This is to say, they serve as a deterrent to ward off sparrows. I think that the Self-Defense Forces, as well, can function effectively as a deterrent, although the Self-Defense Forces cannot attack enemies who are far away.[11]

But in order for the Self-Defense Forces to function as an effective scarecrow, they had to be an effective fighting force. Their capabilities, argued Katō, must at least match those required in the military targets set forth in 1976: "The Air Self-Defense Force ought to have roughly 430 airplanes, the Ground Self-Defense Force ought to have 180,000 personnel, and the Maritime Self-Defense Force ought to have 60 escort ships."

The realists argued that Japan's defense capabilities should be extended to help the United States protect the sea lines of communication extending from Japan through the Strait of Malacca in Southeast Asia.[12] Some of their publications stressed that the vital choke points and the sea lanes connecting them had to be protected at all costs. Therefore, the Self-Defense Forces had to have modern, advanced facilities for surveillance and early warning. That meant acquiring the Airborne Warning and Control System (AWACS).

Yamazaki articulated this new defense strategy in early 1986 by proposing that defense plans and capabilities be based primarily on a strategy of "defense over the sea."[13] He envisaged three stages of defense action by the Self-Defense Forces. First, an early warning system based on AWACS and Over-the-Horizon (OTH) radar would enable the Self-Defense Forces to detect enemy action in the "outer defense zone." In the second stage, the Self-Defense Forces would order interceptors and surface-to-air missiles into action in the "area defense zone." Finally, there would be a third stage, the "point defense zone," where ships, aircraft, and missiles would attack the enemy's strike force before it could launch an assault to invade Japan. This defense strategy required very modern, expensive equipment, and some of it should have offensive military capability. But Yamazaki never mentioned whether this three-stage defense strategy could block an assault on Hokkaido from the north.

To sum up, the realists perceive that the Soviet Union has achieved parity with the United States in nuclear deterrence and had projected greater military power into the Pacific Basin in the seventies. Japan's security is now in jeopardy because its Self-Defense Forces have still not been modernized, while the United States has been scaling down its forces in the Pacific, leaving Japan more vulnerable to attack. These realists share the belief that the U.S.-Japan Security Treaty is of paramount importance to Japan's security. But if that partnership is to continue, Japan has to do its fair share by upgrading its military establishment, especially air and sea surveillance.

The Diplomats

The diplomats comprise former bureaucrats and politicians who are not especially alarmed about Japan's security, to which they see no immediate threat. They argue that Japan's security depends not so much on beefing up the existing Self-Defense Forces as on providing more foreign aid and relying on diplomacy to improve the prospects for regional and global peace. If tensions between the two superpowers could be reduced by diplomacy and by improving the Third World's economies, there would be no need to strengthen Japan's Self-Defense Forces beyond the current defense spending ceiling of 1 percent of GNP.

In mid-1984, Kiichi Miyazawa, leader of a major Liberal Democratic Party (LDP) faction and a candidate for prime minister, proudly stated that Japan had effectively achieved three major goals after World War II: it had become a peace-loving nation, realized democracy, and developed an economic standard of living comparable to that of Western Europe.[14] But Japan still had to make a greater effort to increase its stock of social capital, especially housing. While avoiding an excessive buildup of the military, Japan must continue to make a special effort to increase its social capital. It must eschew the road taken by the United States and the Soviet Union.

> That is why the road which Japan, an economic superpower, has been walking . . . should be the best model for disarmament. No better model can be found, even if we search throughout history. I firmly believe that

a successful walk down this road with confidence will contribute greatly to the international current of disarmament. I think we should advocate this whenever there is an opportunity, and the resources for any excessive military buildup should at least be redirected to assisting the developing countries.

Therefore, Miyazawa strongly argued for a diplomacy of peaceful cooperation:

We should proceed in the direction of making the maximum possible contribution in non-military fields and of taking the initiative in cooperating through peaceful activities by giving the utmost assistance to developing countries, being more active in various UN activities, taking the initiative in large development projects on an international scale, etc.[15]

In early 1986, Saburō Ōkita, a former foreign minister, urged that Japan initiate a Marshall Plan for the heavily indebted countries in Africa.[16] Ōkita pointed out that Japan's defense policy should never be based upon nuclear weapons and that defense spending should remain between 1 and 2 percent of the economy's gross national product (GNP), depending, of course, on the economy's growth rate. Ōkita implied that Japan's Self-Defense Forces were already strong enough and did not require further strengthening.

Former prime minister Takeo Fukuda was interviewed by the Japanese weekly *Economist* in early 1985. He, too, stressed that Japan must never become a big military power and suggested that Japan must do far more in international economic aid than had been the case so far. Fukuda put the argument this way:

I think that the way for Japan to contribute to world peace lies in using its economic power to contribute to the economic, social, and political stabilization of various nations of the world. However, the contribution which Japan is now making to the world with its economic power is still too meager.[17]

Fukuda emphatically rejected any further buildup of the Self-Defense Forces and strongly argued for maintaining the 1 percent of GNP limit on defense spending. He alluded to the new, powerful political pressures demanding that Japan spend more each year for defense. Because there was neither a public consensus nor any political will in government to curb defense spending, Fukuda said, the 1 percent spending limit was necessary to keep defense spending under firm control.

The Conservatives

We use the term conservatives to refer to those members of the Japan Socialist Party (JSP) and other opposition parties that are adamant about preserving the status quo on defense. Intellectuals and security analysts who share this view are also included in this group. The conservatives perceive no external threat to Japan's security. They worry only that new American initiatives might impose new pressures to increase Japan's defense spending. Their main concerns are to keep the Defense Agency under control and to persuade government leaders that the Soviet Union poses no real threat to Japan. Their strategy calls for maintaining the 1 percent ceiling at all costs. They also advocate that the government adhere to its long-standing commitments to the Three Principles of Nuclear Disarmament and Article IX of the Constitution.

Few journals represent this viewpoint better than *Sekai*, a left-wing monthly that strongly appealed to intellectuals in the 1940s and 1950s. *Sekai*'s editors judiciously report on security developments in Japan. Any issue related to Japanese defense or the nation's security is quickly picked up by this journal and examined in considerable detail.[18]

Writing in *Seikai*, the conservatives argue that by the early 1980s the balance of power between the United States and the Soviet Union was nearly even and that the United States could never regain the superiority it had held in the fifties and sixties.[19] Therefore, any efforts by Japan to help the United States guard sea lanes, blockade choke points, and so on would only force the Soviets to speed up their military buildup in Northeast Asia. Further, Japan should avoid siding with the United States in criticizing the Soviet Union and, instead, should be contributing more economic aid to the developing countries.[20] One analyst writing in *Sekai* put it this way:

Although Japan finally achieved her present prosperity after World War II, starting from the worst possible economic conditions, she has paid only a small amount of reparation [to countries occupied in World War II], owing to her arrangements with the U.S., which has been involved in a confrontation with the USSR. Now that Japan is engaged in a wide range of economic activities in the world, she should not explain the international situation in terms of any East-West confrontation, as the Reagan administration does. Further, Japan must make even more positive contributions abroad in the fields of economy and technology, rather than in defense spending, because the economic activities of foreign countries are vital to Japan's existence as a state. Japan must quickly correct these present conditions, where her official development aid (ODA) equals only 0.33 percent of GNP. ODA is very significant as another form of compensation for the war, and Japan has been postponing such repayment.[21]

This argument probably appealed to the guilt feelings that the Japanese people still held about World War II. But more important, the *Sekai* analyst was reiterating the old nonalignment thesis, which pacifists and neutralists had advocated for decades.

The conservatives strongly argue that the 1 percent of gross national product limit on defense spending should never be exceeded. *Sekai* devoted much of its November 1985 issue to the defense budget debates in the Diet and bureaucracy, presenting the familiar "guns versus butter" arguments.[22] Yasuhiro Nagao, another academic, also pointed out that support for the aged and spending for social capital would be adversely affected if defense spending exceeded the 1 percent ceiling.[23]

Some analysts even argued that the Soviets were likely to deploy more long-range missiles with nuclear warheads in Siberia after the United States deployed Tomahawks on its ships. They also contended that the Soviets were strengthening their Northeast Asian defense only because they perceived that U.S.-Chinese relations had improved and the United States was prodding Japan to rearm. The only solution was for the superpowers to negotiate a nuclear freeze and for Japan to adhere strictly to the Three Principles of Nuclear Disarmament.

The conservatives demand that Japan not become involved in the East-West confrontation, maintain a ceiling on defense spending, adhere to the Three Principles of Nuclear Disarmament, and vigorously pursue peace by maintaining a small defense force. They insist that any further buildup of the Self-Defense Forces will merely intimidate the Soviets and further escalate their military buildup.

The Nuclear Advocates

Some experts also argue that Japan should behave as a major state in the international arena by acquiring a nuclear deterrent. They view the Soviet Union as the main threat to Japan's security. Proud of Japan's postwar accomplishments, they urge Japan's leaders to have the political will to provide "real" security for the people. To enhance Japan's security, her leaders must build a powerful defense and a nuclear deterrent. These new policies require that Japan have a political power commensurate with its economic power and that it exercise greater influence in international affairs than heretofore.

While suggesting that Japan ought to have a nuclear deterrent, they also argue that Japan should behave as a responsible power and allocate more economic aid abroad and spend more on research and development for weapons and equipment. Japan is no longer a child in the international community; it has now matured into a healthy adult. Therefore, Japan must take its security obligations more seriously, as the foreign affairs expert Masaaki Sentō writes in the journal *Jiyū*:

It is most urgent that we triple our aid to the developing countries, increase tenfold our expenditures for research and development in defense, and increase our spending on defense equipment two- or threefold. If we do not cast off this dependency behavior, will it not be impossible to resolve friction in the U.S.-Japan defense relationship? Japan is not a twelve-year old child as victorious MacArthur thought, nor a student. Japan has become a healthy adult.[24]

Sentō merely repeated an argument advanced earlier in the summer of 1980 by the pundit Ikutarō Shimizu in a famous article published in *Shokun,* a popular journal.

Shimizu had pointed out that the time had come for Japan to start behaving like the powerful state it really is.[25] In the sixties and seventies, American economic power had begun to decline, just when Japanese economic power had grown. Japan's defense is no longer secure, because the United States can no longer guarantee it. Japan has to find a new source of strength to defend itself. If not, Japan will become more vulnerable to disruption of its foreign trade by an aggressor.[26]

Shimizu then stressed that only the Soviet Union poses any real threat to Japan.[27] In the event of a major war, Japan would be attacked by missiles, by air and sea forces, and finally by amphibious assault. What options for self-defense did Japan have? Japan could strengthen its air and sea surveillance and warning capabilities, but it could not retaliate with sufficient force to deter an aggressor. Shimizu then raises several nuclear options, ideas that had never yet been mentioned. Japan can build its own nuclear weapons; second, Japan could obtain nuclear warheads from the United States for its own delivery vehicles, the approach adopted by West Germany; finally Japan might allow the stationing of U.S. nuclear forces in Japan. Shimizu does not say which option he considers best for Japan.

In the next issue of *Shokun,* Yatsuhirō Nakagawa, a professor at Tsukuba University, refers to Shimizu's options and argues that Japan should ignore the first option but consider the others. Nakagawa stresses that "Japan's nuclear arms must have a convincing retaliatory capability."[28] If not, the strategy would be ineffective. To make his case, he hypothesized two types of nuclear war breaking out between Japan and the Soviet Union.[29] The first scenario, a theater nuclear war, involved an exchange of nuclear warheads destroying a fixed number of Japanese and eastern Russian cities. In this event, Japan would suffer greater damage than the Soviet Union. Nakagawa's second scenario, a strategic nuclear conflict, postulated a larger exchange of nuclear missiles destroying many cities in the Russian heartland and more Japanese cities. Japan had better prospects in this scenario, because she could inflict damage on the Soviets more equivalent to what she might bear. If Japan should opt for the second nuclear deterrent system, she would need three types of nuclear weapons: intercontinental ballistic missiles, sea-launched ballistic missiles, and long-range bombers.

Other experts also mention a nuclear option for Japan. In an exchange with Robert Barnett in January 1983, Kenichi Itō, a professor at Aoyama University, suggests that if the U.S.-Japanese alliance collapsed and Japanese diplomacy with the Soviet Union failed, the Soviet Union would be greatly tempted to attack Japan. Itō then says:

> Japan would have to consider having its own Trident II-type nuclear ballistic missile submarine (SSBN) hiding in the Pacific as its strategic deterrence. However, such security system may involve astronomical costs and isolate Japan from its neighbors, much as happened in the 1930s.[30]

Itō fears that if the United States insists that Japan pay more for its defense, the nuclear option will be the least expensive strategy for Japan to defend itself. His argument was also supported by those who contend that without a nuclear deterrent Japan might not be able to resist Soviet blackmail.

The Strategists

As a group, the strategists perceive a historical and geopolitical threat from the Soviet Union. Yet they are inclined to stress Russian national interest rather than communist ideology as the main factor shaping Moscow's conduct. Consequently, they argue that only force can deter Soviet military power. The strategists also recognize that Moscow has tried to avoid war in the past. But they contend that, no matter how the superpowers deal with each other, Japan should never become a pawn in the superpower conflict. Japan's national interests obviously lie with the West, but Japan should never become an instrument of American policy. The strategists, like the diplomats, prefer strategic-political rather than military means to restrain Moscow. But their perception of the security threat to Japan sets them apart from the diplomats.

The strategists perceive the Soviet Union as *the* major threat to peace and security in East Asia, especially for Japan. For Masamichi Inoki, the former head of the Research Institute for Peace and Security in Tokyo, understanding Soviet diplomacy and military policy depends on one's historical perspective.[31] Inoki contends that the Soviet military buildup in the Far East during the seventies was merely to provide security along her long borders with Communist China and to counter the U.S. military forces in the Pacific Basin. It was difficult to deal with the Soviets, states Inoki, because their leaders never had any self-confidence in their military defense system, believing that only more military power could protect the country. Soviet leadership paranoia and the complex relations between that country's political and military sectors combined to produce tensions that caused military expansionism.[32]

According to Inoki, Japan must meet the Soviet military challenge by increasing its defensive capabilities in antisubmarine warfare, air defense, and rear support capabilities, while strengthening its alliance with the United States. When taking these steps, however, Japan should not appear to threaten the Soviet Union.[33] But Inoki never really explains how such a security policy can overcome Soviet fears about the American-Japanese alliance.

Inoki later argued that the real threat from the Soviet Union was its expansionism in the Third World. Disruption of the oil supply in that geopolitical region would be a calamity for Japan. The Soviet military buildup in the Far East really does not pose as serious a threat to Japan's security as does Soviet Third World expansionism.

Other security analysts like Yōnosuke Nagai depict the Soviet Union as a ruthless, highly rational, and relentlessly expansionist power, yet behaving far differently from Hitler's fascist Germany. The only way Japan can deal with that kind of adversary is to beef up its defense force and always remain militarily prepared.[34]

Masataka Okimiya argues that Japan can meet the Soviet threat by developing a comprehensive security strategy based on certain appropriate domestic and foreign policies.[35] These policies would not be aimed at any particular regional power but at achieving four goals. First, the Self-Defense Forces must be developed on a sound basis. Second, sufficient raw material reserves must be maintained, and rapid economic growth should be sustained by increasing productivity. Third, an adequate civilian defense system—including underground shelters and civil defense organizations—must be established. Finally, Japan's national will must be galvanized so that the people would become strongly committed to the defense of their country. As for Japan's foreign policy, economic and political diplomacy had to be combined in the pursuit of peace. Okimiya's recommendations came roughly five years before the famous Inoki Commission reported its own recommendations to the Japanese government on how Japan should manage its security.[36]

As early as February 1977, Takuya Kubo, former vice-minister of the Defense Agency, the author of the "standard defense force" concept, and chief of the secretariat of the National Defense Council, had urged that a new council was needed for formulating a national security policy. The present office, according to Kubo, was "small in scale" and "unable to handle all areas at one stroke."[37] In fact, Kubo believed that such a council should function like the American National Security Council. Hisahiko Okazaki, a high Foreign Ministry official and a leading strategic thinker, stressed the need for Japan to create a government agency responsible for gathering intelligence,[38] and his ideas were instrumental in establishing a new bureau for that purpose. These organs are no substitute for military power, but the strategists feel that Japan has greater need for intelligence and good political judgment than for additional military hardware.

Other security experts like Makoto Momoi of the National Defense Research Institute argue that Japan should institute policies to achieve three basic conditions for guaranteeing international peace: promoting diplomacy; maintaining the balance of power in East Asia; and preserving the political, social, and economic stability of Japan.[39] Because the Soviet military buildup of the seventies already threatened to tilt the balance of power in the Soviets' favor, Momoi worried that the second condition might not be met. Japan should pay more attention to restoring the pre-1970s conditions, while working hard to fulfill the other two conditions. To achieve those ends, Momoi proposed improving intelligence gathering and interpretation as well as strengthening Japan's capabilities to protect the air and sea around Japan. Even if Japan succeeds in these efforts, Momoi predicts that tensions will arise between Japan and the Soviet Union as the sea lanes become more crowded in the coming decades.

Yōnosuke Nagai, a professor of political science, sees Japan confronted by a new dilemma.[40] So far, Japan has successfully refrained from developing any nuclear weapons or having them deployed in Japan. While moderately armed, Japan has become a world economic power. Yet Japan greatly depends upon other countries for trade, which makes her economy vulnerable. Thus, if a superpower like the United States encounters trade problems with Japan, she can force Japan to make some unpleasant choices.

Nagai points out that Japan is in an advantageous position and should exploit her opportunities to the fullest. Other countries can utilize Japan's industrial-technological potential. Rather than expending more resources on defense, should not Japan serve as a model—a state taking the lead in this world by making international contributions and investments in other countries as well as activating Japan's domestic economy and enhancing her ability to govern? While liberalizing the home markets in banking, insurance, communications, and so on for foreign investment, Japan should increase spending on overseas aid. Finally, Japan must make vigorous diplomatic efforts for world disarmament and global peace. If Japan could accomplish all these things, she would enhance security at home and improve peace abroad.

Nagai's argument is based on an earlier essay he had written, called "The Defense Debate of the Moratorium State."[41] In that essay, Nagai advances two arguments to define the role of the state and its policies in the contemporary age. The first argument calls for a nation to protect its core values (*chūkaku kachi*) "for the sake of its own existence." The second calls for a nation to have "crisis control organizations to cope with any emergency and to survive."

Nagai believes that Yoshida had transformed Japan into a "moratorium state" after World War II, with a new constitution to symbolize the behavior of such a state. Nagai said,

According to Yoshida, the "moratorium" [strategy] meant a period without
state sovereignty under the structure of the Occupation. Paradoxical as it
may seem, Yoshida made full use of this theory of the moratorium state in
order to break away from such a narrow meaning of the "moratorium
situation" in order to achieve true "independence" for Japan. This [strategy]
shows the true worth of Shigeru Yoshida, who was a classical diplomat. For
Yoshida, the economy-is-first policy, the adoption of the new Constitution,
resisting Dulles, and deceiving the Diet to calm any critical situation were
merely tactical means, so that Japan under the Occupation would soon be
able to consolidate its power and become independent of the U.S.[42]

The Yoshida doctrine had worked well, according to Nagai, until the late
seventies, when the United States had begun to press Japan to build up its
defense—putting Japan on notice that time had run out and that it now had to
pay for the protection it had been receiving for so long. What should be Japan's
response to these new pressures and how should Japan manage its security in the
eighties and beyond?

For Nagai, the strategy is clear and simple: continue to apply the concept of
the "moratorium state" in the same flexible way that Yoshida had done decades
before. How would this work? Nagai concedes that the Soviet Union has the
power to easily destroy Japan and that Japan can never muster a defense to deter
Soviet nuclear power. Further, Japan cannot afford to intimidate the Soviets by
resorting to any buildup of her defense, for that would be self-defeating. Japan's
best defense against the Soviet Union is to "compel the Soviet Union not to
have the intent to invade Japan."[43] Japan must never plan to attack the Soviet
Union and must "maintain the minimum-level capability to continue a war in
which Japan would not be defeated."

As for the United States, Nagai points out that in the seventies U.S. military
power had declined, mainly because her leaders failed to initiate new policies to
deal with the severe socioeconomic problems at home. As the global balance of
power shifted, new pressures arose, forcing Japan to mobilize technological and
economic power to reverse that shift. Japan now has new bargaining chips by
which to negotiate with other countries. But what form should that diplomacy
take? Nagai argues that Japan should utilize its economic and technological
power for its long-term national interests, maintain economic relations with all
friendly countries, and preserve international peace. But to carry out the skillful
negotiations necessary to achieve these ends, Japan will have to improve her
diplomatic skills, and that means allocating more domestic resources to train
skilled people for public service.

For the strategists, Japan should adopt a low profile in contributing to the
maintenance of East Asian security and, most important, she should do nothing
that the Soviet Union might perceive as threatening. Japan should undertake
only modest efforts to modernize her Self-Defense Forces and to participate in

joint military exercises with the United States to placate that ally. In this way, Japan can maintain the balance of power between the two superpowers in the Pacific Basin.

Conclusion

Unlike many American analysts reviewing the Japanese scene, we do not regard the nuclear advocacy per se as militarism for two reasons: first, nuclear weapons are suicidal if used against a superpower—they are only a deterrent; second, in principle, it is illogical to argue that Britain, France, China, India, Israel, or Pakistan can have nuclear weapons but Japan cannot.

Japan's few nuclear advocates naturally demand a major-power status for Japan. These voices became heard only after three successive U.S. retreats from Asian countries (Vietnam, South Korea, and the Republic of China on Taiwan) shook Japanese confidence in the permanence of the American nuclear umbrella, and when the United States began to pressure Japan to beef up defense. After the Reagan administration restored Japanese confidence, Japan's nuclear advocates became silent. As of today, as long as the United States maintains the existing security treaty and reassures the Japanese of American resolve, Japan will not choose the nuclear option. That option, if our reading is correct, will have to be imposed on Japan from without through an invasion, dissolution of the security treaty, or its revision. "Japanese militarism" is an old bogey that lives only in American imagination and among the Japanese left.

When these five groups are closely compared, their general perceptions of threats to Japan's security and of how Japan should respond boil down to three broad viewpoints. First, a residue of neutralism still remains in the opposition parties and among their supporters, even though the bulk of the opposition now accepts the Self-Defense Forces. This state of affairs is not necessarily permanent. Recall that Japan's pacifism originated largely as a reaction to America's long military presence in Japan. Strong pacifism will not likely survive if the United States abrogates the alliance and withdraws from Japan.

The second viewpoint, widely shared within the government and the LDP from the mid-1950s until the early 1970s, owes much to Douglas MacArthur and Shigeru Yoshida. Those statesmen insisted on saving the no-war constitution and laying the foundations for America to defend Japan. The constitution enabled Japan to enjoy American protection without paying too heavily for it. It was the tacit cooperation of Yoshida and the neutralists that helped preserve MacArthur's ideal of a disarmed Japan. Today, most policymakers accept the U.S.-Japan alliance and simply want to improve that relationship.

The general arguments of the diplomats, the strategists, and many of the realists can be translated into political action in the following way. Japan should spend slightly more than 1 percent of gross national product for defense each year to modernize the sea and air surveillance and defense capabilities of the Self-Defense Forces. Those forces should also cooperate more closely with the U.S. military forces, but again only on a limited basis. Japan should still refrain from allowing nuclear weapons to be openly deployed in Japan and should not acquire any for herself. Finally, Japan should engage in international diplomatic and economic activities for peace, but as a follower rather than assuming any active leadership role. This view of national security requires that Japan continue to perform the same balancing act she has done in previous decades: neither build a large defense that would intimidate Japan's neighbors, nor offend her powerful ally, the United States.

The third and final viewpoint is based on the argument that Japan should assume a larger security role in East Asia, deal with the United States on a basis of equivalence, and spend far more each year to develop a powerful military defense. Advocates of this viewpoint include the nuclear advocates and some realists. They can be found in the LDP, but they are still a minority. Some of the most pro-American and activist prime ministers, such as Kishi and Nakasone, are presumed to subscribe to this view. This viewpoint receives no support from the major newspapers or from the public at the moment. Yet it is an outlook that will command increasing respect in the years ahead if the United States, beset by trade and fiscal deficits, reassesses its relationship with Japan.

Our review of the debate over Japanese security between 1978 and 1986 clearly indicates that America must not equate a more self-reliant Japan with militarism. The impulses to revive the pre-war imperial-military system are non-existent. Yet a stronger Japan will exude some nationalism as a matter of course, and nationalism always remains a latent force, as in most countries. But for the moment, the mainstream view in Japan appears to be a refinement of the Yoshida doctrine.

Notes

1. Osamu Kaihara *et al.*, "This Is Japan's Defense Power," *Shukan Yomiuri*, March 5, 1978, cited in *Summaries of Selected Japanese Magazines (SSJM)*, translated by the Political Section of the American Embassy, Tokyo, March 1978, p. 33.

2. Takio Yamazaki, "'Kekkan' jieitai to shiteki sarete" [The Self-Defense Forces Have Been Singled Out as Defective], *Jiyu*, August 1980, pp. 67–68.

3. Kazuhisa Ogawa, *Zai Nichi Beigun* [U.S. Forces in Japan] (Tokyo: Kodansha, 1985), Chapters 5 and 6.

4. Hiroyuki Maruyama, "Soren Taiheiyo kantai o keikai seyo" [Take Heed of the Soviet Pacific Fleet], *Shokun*, November 1985, p. 101.

5. Takio Yamazaki, "Nihon no anzen o do iji suruka" [How To Maintain Japan's Security?], *Jiyu*, May 1980, pp. 130–131.

6. Ibid., p. 132. See also his article "Jiyū to dokuritsu o mamoru bōeiryoku" [Defense Power for Preserving Freedom and Independence], *Jiyū*, December 1980, p. 114.

7. Osamu Miyoshi, "Chūritsu Nihon ka, shin Nichi-Bei dōmei ka" [A Neutral Japan or a New Japan-U.S. Alliance?], *Chūō Kōron*, March 1980, pp. 96–100.

8. Jōji Ōmura and Shinkichi Etō, "80 nendai no bōei mondai ni dō taiō suruka" [How To Deal with the Defense Problem of the 1980s?], *Bungei Shunjū*, November 1980, pp. 369–370.

9. Hideaki Kase, "Nihon rettō no bōei seimeisen" [The Defense Lifeline of the Japanese Archipelago], *Jiyū*, January 1979, pp. 18–25, especially pp. 23–24.

10. Shigeki Nishimura, "Developing Outlook on Soviet Moves; Soviet Union, Substance of Potential Threat; Epoch-Making Discussion Clarifying Ambiguous Argument on Soviet Threat," *SSJM*, December 1985, p. 8.

11. Kōichi Katō, "Bōei shomondai no kontei ni hisomu mono" [Factors Hidden at the Roots of the Various Defense Problems], *Bungei Shunjū*, August 1985, p. 199.

12. Kenichi Kitamura, "Taiheiyō shirein no anzen hoshō to kokusai kyōryoku" [International Cooperation and the Security of the Pacific Sea Lanes], *Sekai to Nihon*, December 25, 1983, pp. 8–49; "Shirein bōeiron" [An Essay on the Defense of the Sea Lanes], presented to the Special Committee on Security of the Upper House of the Diet Discussing the Problems and Characteristics of the Defense of the Sea Lanes (April 11, 1983).

13. Yamazaki, "Nihon no anzen o dō iji suruka," p. 74.

14. Interview of Kiichi Miyazawa by Masataka Kosaka, "Watashi no shisan baizōron—dai niji keizai hiyaku to heiwa kyōryoku gaikō" [My Plank for Doubling Property: The Second Economic Leap and the Diplomacy of Peaceful Cooperation], *Bungei Shunjū*, July 1984, pp. 94–95.

15. Ibid., p. 104.

16. An interview with Saburō Ōkita, "Time for a Japanese Marshall Plan?" *Look Japan*, January 10, 1986, pp. 2–3.

17. Takeo Fukuda, "Senzen no kurai michi o ayundewa naranai" [Don't Walk the Dark Prewar Path], *Ekonomisuto*, October 8, 1985, p. 27.

18. *Sekai* has the distinction of having spearheaded Japan's neutralist movement in the days when George F. Kennan was at the State Department and contemplating a neutral Japan. See Takeshi Igarashi, *Tai-Nichi kowa to reisen: sengo Nichi-Bei kankei no keisei* [Peace with Japan and the Cold War: The Formation of Postwar Japan-U.S. Relations] (Tokyo: Tokyo University Press, 1986), pp. 230–267.

19. Kenichi Nakamura, "Soren kyōiron kara no dakkyakyu" [Extricating Ourselves from the Thesis of Soviet Threat], *Sekai*, April 1985, pp. 71–72.

20. Takeshi Igarashi, "Heiwa no kōso: shin no kokusaiteki sekinin towa nanika" [The Concept of Peace: What is Our True International Responsibility?], *Sekai*, April 1985, p. 20.

21. Ibid., pp. 40–41.

22. See *Sekai*, November 1985, pp. 10–116.

23. Yasuhirō Nagao, "Dare ga futan surunoka" [Who Bears the Burden?], *Sekai*, November 1985, pp. 76–77.

24. Masaaki Sentō, "Nihon wa 'gakuwari kokka' de aru: tenki no Nichi-Bei bōei masatsu o kangeru" [Japan Is a Dependent State: A Review of Japan-U.S. Defense Friction at a Turning Point], *Jiyū*, October 1983, p. 109.

25. Ikutarō Shimizu, "Kaku no sentaku: Nihon yo kokka tare" [The Nuclear Option: Japan, Be a State!], *Shokun*, July 1980, pp. 22–68.

26. Ibid., p. 93.

27. "Nihon ga motsubeki bōeiryoku" [The Defense Power Japan Ought To Have], ibid., part II, pp. 75–79.

28. Yatsuhirō Nakagawa, "Kaku no mochikomi igai no michi wa nai" [There Is No Other Way Except To Have a Nuclear Power Introduced], *Shokun*, September 1980, p. 62.

29. Ibid., pp. 84–85.

30. Robert W. Barnett, *Beyond War: Japan's Concept of Comprehensive National Security* (Washington: Pergamon Press, 1984), p. 87.

31. Masamichi Inoki, "Soren no 'kyōi' ni dō taisho suruka" [How To Cope with the Soviet Threat], *Chūō Kōron*, November 1976, pp. 56–58.

32. Ibid., pp. 62–64.

33. Masamichi Inoki, "Bōei rongi no kyojitsu" [The Truth and Fallacies of the Defense Controversy], *Chūō Kōron*, January 1981, p. 117.

34. Yōnosuke Nagai, "Nihon gaikō ni okeru 'shizen' to 'sakui'" [Naturalness and Artificiality in Japan's Diplomacy], *Chūō Kōron*, June 1982, p. 89.

35. Masataka Okimiya, "Sōgō anzen hoshō eno teigen" [A Proposal for a Comprehensive Security], *Shin Bōei Ronshū*, March 1974, pp. 1–22.

36. Masamichi Inoki and Masataka Kōsaka (eds.), *Nihon no anzen hoshō to bōei eno kinkyū teigen* [Some Urgent Proposals for the Security of Japan and Its Defenses] (Tokyo: Kōdansha, 1982).

37. Takuya Kubo, "Kokubō kaigi no kyōka o" [Strengthening the National Defense Council], *Ekonomisuto*, February 15, 1977, p. 40.

38. Hisahiko Okazaki, "Ima koso jimae no senryaku teki shikō o" [Now Is the Time for Our Own Strategic Thought], *Bungei Shunjū*, March 1986, p. 110.

39. Makoto Momoi, "Nihon no 'sōgō' anzen hoshō o kangaeru: 80-nendai ni nami takamaru Taiheiyō eno taiō" [Considering Japan's 'Comprehensive' Security: Coping with the Pacific as the Waves Mount Higher in the 1980s], *Keieisha*, August, 1979, pp. 28–29.

40. Yōnosuke Nagai, "Nihon gaikō ni okeru 'shizen' to 'sakui'," p. 89.

41. Yōnosuke Nagai, "Moratoriamu kokka no bōeiron" [The Defense Debate of the Moratorium State], *Chūō Kōron*, January 1981, pp. 74–108.

42. Ibid., p. 79.

43. Ibid., p. 84.

4

The Press and Public Opinion

The Japanese press has long exerted a powerful influence on the thinking of government officials and their policies, especially toward national security. Although the strength of the left and the center-left has compelled Japan to have small Self-Defense Forces, public opinion changed in the late seventies and eighties to supporting the Japan-U.S. alliance and the modest improvement of the military. Of the five major daily newspapers, only the *Asahi* and the *Mainichi* are still critical of government efforts to increase defense spending and develop closer security ties with the United States.

The Press and Public Opinion Before 1979

By the early eighties, 125 newspapers were distributed nationwide, regionally, and locally, with a total circulation of 68 million copies.[1] The top five newspapers are *Yomiuri Shimbun*, with around 8.7 million in circulation; *Asahi Shimbun*, with 7.5 million; *Mainichi Shimbun*, with 4.6 million; *Sankei Shimbun*, with 2.0 million; and *Nihon Keizai Shimbun*, with 1.8 million.[2] *Yomiuri's* circulation alone surpasses that of the *New York Times*, the *Washington Post*, the *Wall Street Journal*, the *Christian Science Monitor* and the *New York Daily News* combined.[3] These and other newspapers produce a circulation higher than one paper for every two people, compared to less than one paper for every three people in the United States.[4]

Japan's worldwide network of correspondents totaled over 400 by 1982, with the greatest number serving in Europe, North America, and Asia.[5] In the sixties and seventies, the top three newspapers were generally left of center when reporting the news.[6] They have been more critical of the United States than of the Soviet Union, more sympathetic toward the People's Republic of China (PRC) and North Vietnam, and especially critical of their home government on U.S.-Japanese security relations and spending for defense.

In the sixties and early seventies, the Soviet Union tried to negotiate with Japan a treaty that would finalize World War II, resolve the dispute over the four islands north of Hokkaido (called the Northern Territories), and develop agreements to facilitate more Japanese investment in Siberia and economic cooperation between both countries. The Japanese press typically reported Soviet-Japanese relations in a conciliatory manner, expressed a guarded optimism that agreements were possible, and invariably qualified that optimism by noting that if only more vigorous efforts could be made by both parties, particularly on Tokyo's part, then Soviet-Japanese relations would improve.

For example, on December 20, 1972, *Mainichi* stated that "relations between Japan and the Soviet Union have now entered a stage where they need a treaty basis."[7] The *Mainichi* said,

> Japan-Soviet relations have been piling up goodwill in the past 15 years. However, we have now entered a new state, and past ways are no longer adequate. In economic relations, strong cooperative relations will be needed in the future. From now on, mammoth projects must be carried out, based on the development of oil and natural gas.[8]

Just as the press was uncritical of the Soviet position while critically reviewing their government's diplomacy, the major dailies also avoided any harsh reporting about the People's Republic of China (PRC) and North Vietnam.

The Japanese press corps in the PRC frequently refused even to print news that it normally reported from other countries, because of fear that the Chinese Communist authorities might be offended. Japanese journalists engaged in a conspiracy of silence when they did not report the downfall of Lin Piao. After the foreign press began speculating on Lin's demise, Japanese journalists still remained silent or even ignored such speculations. Finally, when the evidence became overwhelming, "a Japanese correspondent was reported to have told his Tokyo office that there was no doubt about the downfall of Lin Piao and that the Tokyo office should feel free thenceforth to use Agence France Presse dispatches datelined Peking without hesitation."[9] Again, take the example of a massive riot that occurred in Hangchow (Chekiang province) in 1975. *Asahi* fully knew that some 200,000 workers, in defiance of the government, had battled with troops for several months. Rather than report this event, *Asahi* merely introduced a brief Agence France Presse report about it. Neither reports from its correspondents nor any editorials or commentaries ever appeared in *Asahi*.[10]

While behaving in a subservient manner toward the PRC, the press was critical of its own government when reporting on the normalizing of relations between the two countries. Long before the Japan-China Aviation Agreement was concluded in 1974, the press "asserted that the agreement should and could be reached through greater effort on the part of the Japanese government."[11] Some dailies went so far as to declare that the aviation agreement should have been settled along the lines demanded by the PRC. A *Yomiuri* editorial argued on December 7, 1973, that it was hardly proper to have no air link between the PRC and Japan when Japan Airlines had thirty-seven weekly flights to Taiwan. The editorial then scolded the government for deviating from the basic spirit of the Japan-China Joint Communiqué of some months before.[12] Virtually every newspaper maintained the position that the demands from Beijing were just and that Japan had no basis for disagreement.

Finally, dailies like *Asahi* argued that Japan's normalization with Beijing was justified at any cost. *Asahi's* reason was that, in polls of its readers, a majority agreed that there was only one China and that the PRC government represented China. A good example of *Asahi's* activities occurred in mid-1972 when Prime Minister Eisaku Sato announced his resignation from office. On June 7, an *Asahi* correspondent in Beijing filed a story suggesting that any new prime minister must "accept Beijing's three principles for normalization and must demonstrate, by concrete action, that its pledge to do so was genuine."[13] The correspondent even argued that if Takeo Fukuda became the new prime minister it would be most difficult for Japan to normalize relations with China. *Asahi* might have believed that this kind of reporting was justified because its readers would support it, but the public's view of the China normalization issue might have been more complex than that held by *Asahi's* readers. Other newspaper polls revealed that a majority of those polled preferred to maintain relations with the Republic of China on Taiwan while recognizing the government of China.[14]

Just as Japanese press reports of the PRC were biased and partisan, so were press reports about the Vietnam War. In November 1983, the prestigious *Bungei Shunjū* presented a dialogue between two distinguished Japanese journalists, both winners of important literary prizes: Koichi Kondō of *Sankei Shimbun* and Yoshihisa Komori of *Mainichi*. Their remarks revealed that Japanese newspapers were out of touch with the reality of the war in Vietnam and that Japanese newspapers had completely misreported the war. No Japanese writer ever refuted their main points after the *Bungei Shunjū* article had appeared.

Kondō and Komori claimed that Japanese newspapers had described the so-called liberation struggle in the south as having "spontaneously originated only among the people in the south" and that the northern regime had sent only materiel, never people or troops, into the south to wage war.[15] They pointed out that overwhelming evidence existed at the time proving that the north had transferred a large number of armed personnel into the south. Without that crucial support, the Viet Cong could not have survived and weakened the southern government.

They mentioned that Japanese newspapers never referred to the anti-Saigon government forces as "communist," instead using the term "liberation forces."[16] The Japanese press never reported that North Vietnam had dispatched troops into the south. By failing to inform the Japanese public of the truth, they tacitly supported Hanoi propaganda. Komori had even visited the "liberated" base areas in the south and observed North Vietnamese soldiers and Soviet-made weapons, including tanks, in use. Moreover, nearly all Japanese journalists reported the fall of Saigon as the "liberation" of Saigon.[17] The press never mentioned that an independent state had been defeated and taken over by a communist state. Nor did the press discuss this new communist expansion in Southeast Asia and its implications for the peace and security of the region.

Given the strong left-of-center views of the major dailies, how did they report national security affairs in the early 1970s? Various papers reported that their polls showed the public was far more concerned about "bread and butter" issues than about Japan's defense or the size and quality of the Self-Defense Forces.[18] The press also stated that annual defense spending should be limited. On November 30, 1970, for example, *Sankei* argued that the government and the Defense Agency should establish a clear upper limit to defense spending and provided a rationale for it:

> Taking all these circumstances into consideration, we cannot but feel that the SDFs are only trying to keep pace with the armed forces of other countries, without studying a proper upper limit or re-examining their own foundations. We think that an attitude of the Self-Defense Forces has caused misunderstanding both at home and abroad.[19]

Several years later, the 1 percent of GNP spending cap became the rallying point for the press and other critics to restrain defense spending.

In February 1971, *Asahi* reported that Kawasaki Heavy Industries was about to export V-107 helicopters and that Mitsubishi Heavy Industries intended to sell two-engine turboprop MUs to the Swedish air force. *Asahi* severely criticized such steps as violating the government's arms export ban.[20] *Asahi* condemned weapons exports as "dangerous moves" and demanded strict adherence to the government's ban.

The hostility of the press toward Japan's defense was again demonstrated in the fall of 1972, when the National Defense Council's chief of secretariat, Osamu Kaihara, stated publicly, first at home and then in Washington, that Japan's defense was inadequate against any attack from outside and that the Self-Defense Forces could not be expected to assist the United States elsewhere in the Pacific because they simply did not possess the capacity to do so.[21] Rather than critically review whether Kaihara was right and the defense system was inadequate, the press merely recruited commentators to discuss whether Japan had any need for defense at all.[22] In other words, the major dailies consistently criticized government policies on defense.

The Public's Attitude Toward Security Before 1975

What was public opinion like toward defense? From 1951 to the early 1970s, well over 40 percent of the Japanese people surveyed by opinion polls expressed a desire for Japan to have a military force.[23] As for rearming Japan, however, opinion polls revealed that during the 1950s around 42 percent polled were against Japan undertaking any rearmament efforts[24] and that between 1955 and 1972 well over 50 percent polled were against Japan acquiring any nuclear weapons.[25] In 1950, only 39 percent wanted Japan to have a military, but the proportion of the public supporting a military was undoubtedly smaller between 1945 and 1949 and probably had begun to climb when the Korean War erupted.

Yet the public did express during the 1960s and early 1970s a willingness to have Japan slowly expand the Self-Defense Forces. The percentage of those polled expressing their support rose from 58 percent in 1956 to 73 percent in 1974. But when people were polled from 1955 to 1970 on their views about revising Article IX of the constitution, well over 40 percent responded that they were opposed to any constitutional revision.[26]

Meanwhile, the public's support for the U.S.-Japan Security Treaty fell from a high approval rating of 80 percent in 1951 to an all-time low of 20 percent in 1960, the year of the massive riots in Tokyo and other cities to oppose ratification of the revised treaty. But public approval for the security treaty gradually rose in the late 1960s, with around one-third of the public voicing support for it by the mid-1970s.[27] Slightly less than one-third opposed the treaty, and roughly 40 percent did not have a firm opinion.

Meanwhile, the public's approval rating for the United States remained high in the early 1960s, but after 1965 it began to decline from a high of 41 percent to a low of 22 percent in 1975.[28] Yet the proportion of the public that expressed a dislike for America rose only slightly during these same years and in 1975 was only 8 percent, compared to 6 percent in 1960, the height of public protests against the security treaty.

When taken together, these polls show that a majority of the Japanese from the 1950s until the early 1970s favored Japan having a small military force. Furthermore, a majority of the public opposed any revision of Article IX of the constitution. A small majority still were undecided as to whether they liked the U.S.-Japan Security Treaty, but a solid one-third supported the treaty.

Did the frequent anti-American views expressed in the major newspapers influence the public's attitude toward the United States? It would seem not. The press was unable to convince people to oppose the government's efforts to maintain a small Self-Defense Force in the 1960s and 1970s. The press was unwilling to endorse any government efforts to bolster the Self-Defense Force in those years, yet the majority of the people approved of Japan at least having them. But the public certainly did not want them strengthened in any dramatic way. Therefore, the press and public opinion were probably not far apart on issues related to national security.

The Press and Public Opinion After 1975

By late 1979, four major developments in Asia had caused great anxiety in Japan: (1) the buildup of Soviet military forces on Shikotan Island in the Northern Territories; (2) the expansion of the Soviet fleet in the Pacific; (3) the invasion of Afghanistan by Soviet troops and armor; and (4) the decline of U.S. power as revealed in the Watergate affair and the retreats from Vietnam, South Korea, and the Republic of China on Taiwan. These developments sparked the great debate over Japan's security already described in Chapter 3. It was in this new context of changing perceptions and public debate that public opinion gradually became more supportive of spending more for defense and maintaining the U.S.-Japan security relationship.

Moscow's decision to build an airfield and deploy a large contingent of troops and advanced jet fighters on Shikotan alarmed Tokyo and shook the confidence of those who had long regarded the Soviet Union as posing no threat to Japan. Various statements made by the press in September 1979 clearly indicate that for the first time a new point of view was being articulated about the Soviet Union. *Yomiuri* offered this reaction on September 28, 1979:

> As for the Japanese people, who renounced war as a means of settling international disputes, constructing a base is extremely hard to understand. We must say that such behavior only produces those effects that will delight people who advocate "the threat from the north." . . . These islands are places which the Soviet Union once promised to return. We cannot condone the Soviet Union's construction of military bases there and exercising its control. The Japanese government ought to express its view by a clear protest.[29]

Mainichi and *Nihon Keizai* expressed similar alarm, even urging the Foreign Ministry to express Japan's displeasure and demand a reply from Moscow.[30]

Several months later, newspapers reported on new Soviet naval vessels in the northern Pacific.[31] The aircraft carrier *Minsk* had just been assigned to the Soviet Pacific fleet, which already had 770 ships capable of sailing to different Soviet bases as far away as South Yemen and Vietnam.

Then, on December 27, 1979, the Soviet Union invaded Afghanistan, claiming it had responded to a request for help from the beleaguered Marxist-Leninist government that had recently seized power in Kabul. Japanese editorials denounced the act. *Asahi* took the moral high ground, appealed to the principle

that nations should respect the sovereignty of other states, and expressed concern
that Moscow-Tokyo relations might be harmed.

> Japan absolutely cannot approve the Soviets' having deployed armed forces
> in large quantities to a sovereign nation for the purpose of attaining its
> political purpose regardless of what reasons and background situation there
> are. . . . It is important to stress to the Soviet Union that the majority of
> the Japanese people oppose [the Soviet invasion of Afghanistan], and at
> the same time to take care so that Japan-Soviet relations as a whole will
> not come to naught, due to this problem.[32]

Other papers like *Nihon Keizai* took a much tougher stance by pointing out that
the Soviet Union never hesitated to use force when it was in that country's
interest to do so.

> As shown in the current invasion of Afghanistan, it is confirmed once
> again that the Soviet Union does not hesitate to use military force in the
> peripheral areas near the Soviet Union, which are strategically important,
> no matter how big the tangible and intangible price may be.[33]

Yomiuri denounced the invasion by stating, "It is a terrifying abuse of a
friendship and good neighborliness treaty."[34] Of all the papers reporting the
affair, *Asahi* clearly adopted the softest stance, merely expressing disapproval in
a conciliatory tone.

Since 1980, other events also contributed to a new concern in Japan that all
was not right in the international sphere: the downing of a Korean Airline
jetliner in August 1983; the growing strength of communist rebel activities in
the Philippines after the assassination of Benigno Aquino in Manila in August
1983; the bombing deaths of several key South Korean political leaders in
Burma at the hands of North Korean terrorists in October 1983; the breakdown
of arms negotiations between Washington and Moscow between November
1983 and January 1985; the outburst of terrorist activity in the Middle East after
1981; and the 1984 refusal of New Zealand to receive port-of-call visits from
American aircraft carriers equipped with nuclear weapons. All these events were
viewed with an alarm and urgency not observable in previous decades.

One of the major dailies, *Yomiuri,* began to shift. *Yomiuri* adopted a more
centrist position, became more critical of Marxist-Leninist regimes, and refused
to condone their military expansionism. It warned its readers in January 1984 of
the necessity of realizing that Soviet military power was rapidly expanding in
the Pacific Basin and that they should be aware of the need to deter this new
buildup.

> Can we close our eyes to the open threat by the USSR toward Japan, and
> say that the argument holding the U.S. to be the source of the military

buildup is impartial? Many who are denying the theories of "deterrence and balance" and of "the Soviet threat" are advocating the leftist strategy of anti-U.S., pro-Soviet.[35]

In fact, *Yomiuri* criticized Japanese left-wing support of Marxist-Leninist regimes and their attacks upon the United States. In early 1984 it warned its readers in this way:

> What should be guarded against in particular is the inclination towards the left wing. Today, those with a left-wing inclination never refer to themselves as "leftist." They try to hide it behind words like peace, arms reduction, and opposition to nuclear weapons which sound well to the ears of the general public.[36]

Some newspapers like *Sankei* even criticized the organized efforts by radicals and pacifists to demonstrate against the arrival of U.S. naval ships in Japanese ports. In mid-1984, *Sankei* urged its readers to recognize that the international situation had worsened for Japan and that Japan should honor such visits.

> There presently is an infantile opposition movement among some in our country in connection with port-calls by U.S. ships carrying nuclear weapons, inclusive of the issue of the deployment of Tomahawks. However, this is complacency ignoring the international reality and common sense, depending on others for security and refusing to bear our . . . share of joint responsibility.[37]

Yet *Asahi* and *Mainichi* still had not expressed any deep sense of concern about the Soviet Union and its growing power in Asia. They merely appealed to the government to redouble its diplomatic efforts along with other peace-loving countries to reach agreements with the Soviet Union so that the balance of power could be maintained. The following statement by *Asahi* in late 1984 conveys that newspaper's assessment of the Soviet Union.

> A cool-headed analysis of the intentions of the Soviet Union, which is pushing the strengthening of its military power, is also necessary; and it also goes without saying that diplomatic efforts are needed to prevent this "threat" from becoming manifest.[38]

Mainichi, too, recognized the new Soviet military buildup in Cam Ranh Bay and elsewhere, warning its readers that "we cannot but feel a so-called threat from the Soviet Union."[39] But neither *Asahi* nor *Mainichi* ever urged the strengthening of the U.S.-Japan security alliance or creating a new regional security alliances to meet this new danger.

To show their great concern about the Soviet military buildup in the Pacific Basin, newspapers like *Sankei* and *Yomiuri* devoted more attention to discussing whether the Self-Defense Forces were really equipped to contribute to the overall balance of power in the North Pacific. In fact, they even tacitly advocated a new role the Defense Agency might have to play in the mid-1980s, a role that may require greatly strengthening the air and sea defenses of Japan. In early August 1985, *Yomiuri* made this remark:

> The military situation around Japan is becoming more tense, as can be seen also in the strengthening of the Soviet Far East Forces. In view of this situation, the Defense Agency regards the strengthening of its air defense at sea, around Japan, and its defense of the sea lanes as its biggest goal.[40]

This was the first instance of a major daily newspaper calling for more action in sea lane defense. *Yomiuri* began to devote more discussion to how the Self-Defense Forces were improving their defense capabilities.[41]

Although *Yomiuri, Sankei,* and *Nihon Keizai* began expressing alarm at the new Soviet military buildup, *Asahi* and *Mainichi* have remained highly critical of the LDP and any efforts on its part to build up the Self-Defense Forces. In fact, as Yoshihisa Komori has pointed out in the following examples, the top two dailies were reluctant to see Japan build up its military.

> Some members of the government and the LDP are shaking the Ministry of Finance up to demand a special treatment for defense expenditures. We oppose stoutly the idea of making defense spending a "sanctuary". . . . It is obvious to everyone that the current domestic situation makes it impossible for the Defense Agency's budgetary request to be approved as the actual defense budget. . . . If Prime Minister Suzuki breaks his pledge not to make the defense budget a "sanctuary," this sanctuary will be bound to expand endlessly. (*Mainichi*, December 8, 1980)

> While we fully recognize that the U.S.-Japanese Security Treaty is the foundation of U.S.-Japanese relations and plays an important role for Japan's security, we do not consider the international situation surrounding Japan, particularly the Soviet military buildup in East Asia, so threatening as to demand defense expenditures above the present level. Given the state of the Japanese people's standard of living and sentiment, the fiscal year 1981 defense budget of 2.4 trillion yen (10.9 billion dollars) is already excessive. It is even astonishing that a nation that renounced war by its Constitution has come to possess the eighth largest military power in the world. It is feared that further increases in Japan's military power will heighten the tension in East Asia. . . . We feel it is an urgent task for Japan, as a peaceable nation, to expeditiously establish a path to international cooperation. (*Mainichi,* November 3, 1981)

The LDP national convention adopted a new policy guideline that gives the top priority to the effort to strengthen national defense. We entertain serious apprehensions about it. . . . This policy guideline lacks a viewpoint to promote Japan's own peace strategy. If implemented, it will likely lead Japan down the path of unrestricted military buildup. (*Asahi,* January 16, 1982)[42]

These dailies also strongly argued for limiting defense spending to 1 percent of gross national product and adhering to the constitution.

But at the same time, *Yomiuri* bristled at the U.S. Congress's proposal to impose a defense tax as an infringement on Japan's sovereignty, in an editorial on November 15, 1981.

It is hard to understand attempts in the [United States] Congress to pass resolutions demanding another sovereign nation's defense expenditure increase. The idea of collecting a "security tax" from Japan is even impertinent. . . . Although most Japanese seem to perceive the Soviet threat just about the same way the United States does, they do not support a policy of impetuous military buildup. It is obvious that pressuring them heavily would only produce an adverse reaction.[43]

In late 1983, *Mainichi* also grumbled about the recent increase in Japan's defense spending: "It is impermissible to let our self-defense power deviate from the scope of our Constitution."[44] In late August 1985, *Asahi* stated that "the problem of the 1 percent ceiling also contains elements running counter to the spirit of our peace Constitution, stepping out of the framework of strict adherence to defense, and running counter to the Three Principles of Nuclear Disarmament."[45]

But *Sankei* advocated abandoning the long-standing rule of Premier Miki's ceiling on defense spending. It urged "that defense spending must be permitted to increase beyond the ceiling of one percent if need be, in order to achieve" the goal of realizing Japan's 1976 National Defense Program Outline.[46]

The top three dailies also strongly criticized any U.S. attempts to urge Japan to increase its defense spending and vigorously demanded that the Japanese government resist these pressures. On February 13, 1982, a *Mainichi* editorial commented on the letter from sixty-eight members of the U.S. House of Representatives to Prime Minister Suzuki calling for Japan to raise its defense spending above the level of 1 percent of gross national product:

One way to respond to the letter is for us to assert that this type of request for a stronger defense will only cause a backlash among the Japanese. In fact, some already complain that this is an act of interference in Japan's internal affairs. . . . Needless to say, what constrains Japan's defense is our Constitution and the Japanese people's consensus that the situation around

Japan is not so pressing as to require its revision. Why was the Constitution that advocates peace born? Why has it come to take its deep roots in Japan? The Prime Minister's urgent task is to vigorously gain an international recognition for the Constitution.[47]

Moreover, the top three dailies also remained very critical of President Reagan's strong defense buildup during his administration and of U.S. policy in general toward Japan's defense.[48]

Since the late 1970s, Japan's opposition parties also toned down their former opposition to alliance with the United States and to bolstering Japan's defense establishment. But two leading newspapers, *Asahi* and *Mainichi,* the bellwethers of media and public opinion, still carry on the early postwar tradition of opposing the government. They continue to wage a dogged rear-guard struggle with the ruling party. For example, they have criticized the Ministry of Education's history textbooks describing Japan's role in World War II and faulted former Prime Minister Nakasone's intention to visit the Yasukuni Shrine to honor Japan's war dead as general "peace" issues. The defection of *Yomiuri* from the ranks of the big three was a major change. But *Asahi* continues to play to the center-left, a stance undoubtedly calculated to elicit foreign as well as domestic attention. *Asahi* appears to furnish the news that the *New York Times* began to use as part of its anti-Nakasone, antimilitarist reporting in the mid-1980s.[49]

Public opinion surveys show that between 1978 and 1984, when the debate over Japan's defense grew intense, a modest increase in public concern about the country's security did take place. Between 1981 and 1984, for example, there was a modest growth (from 36 to 42 percent) of concern over the Soviet Union shifting more troops to the Northern Territories. There was also an increase from 36 to 41 percent in the number of those expressing concern about the balance of power between the Soviet Union and the United States.[50]

Between 1978 and 1984, the polls showed a gradual increase (from 47.7 to 50.3 percent) in the combined share of population moderately and highly concerned about Japan's security.[51] This gradual increase most likely reflected the greater coverage given to Japan's defense by the press and popular magazines. In 1975, 1981, and 1984, the percentages of those who approved of the government's gradual increase of defense spending within 1 percent of gross national product were 47, 47, and 54 percent, respectively.[52]

Moreover, there was a slight increase in the number of those who believe that the true function of the Self-Defense Forces is to deter aggression and protect the nation's security. This figure rose from 56 percent in 1978 to 59 percent in 1981 and to 63 percent in 1984.[53] Similarly, there was an increase in the number of those who believe that the best means to preserve Japan's security is for the military to be maintained at its current spending level under the U.S.-Japan Security Treaty. This figure rose from 54 percent in 1975 to 64 percent in 1981 and finally to 69 percent in 1984.[54]

These findings suggest that roughly two out of every three adult Japanese favor the security treaty and the gradual buildup of the Self-Defense Forces. But public opinion continues to uphold the 1 percent ceiling. On March 17, 1985, *Asahi* reported that 58 percent of the respondents polled insisted on keeping it.[55] On February 25, 1987, *Mainichi* reported that 77 percent of its respondents wanted to keep it.[56]

Despite the gradual increase in public support in the early 1980s for the government's efforts to expand the Self-Defense Forces, there never occurred any major shifts in public opinion on the defense issue. The majority of the public has been content with the LDP's defense spending policy.

Conclusion

It is fashionable to be antimilitarist in Japan today. This should not be equated with the neutralism of the early postwar years. Rather, this sentiment represents direct support for the LDP establishment, which adheres to the revised Yoshida policy. The Japanese media and public are convinced that Japan's success stems from its policy of not squandering resources on arms, and that America's difficulties stem from its own massive arms expenditures. The Japanese media may sound utopian at times, but this is a calculated stance. The Japanese cannot really get serious about defense because of the structure of their alliance, of which the Americans are the mainstay. This structure rests on the assumption that a rearmed Japan would be a menace to its neighbors. So, with the help of their liberal foreign counterparts, Japan's media retain the bogey of Japanese militarism and put it to good use. To exhort the Japanese to spend more on defense will be futile as long as America stands in awe of that bogey.

Notes

1. Nihon Shimbun Kyūkai Staff, *The Japanese Press, 1983* (Tokyo: Japan Newspaper Publishers' and Editors' Association, 1983), p. 14.

2. Kōdansha Staff, *Kōdansha Encyclopedia of Japan* (Tokyo: Kōdansha Ltd., 1983), p. 51.

3. Yoshihisa Komori, "The Role of the Press in Japanese Government Decision-Making on Defense" (a draft copy of a prepared statement to a workshop sponsored by the House Foreign Affairs Committee, Subcommittee on Asian and Pacific Affairs; the Woodrow Wilson International Center for Scholars; and the Congressional Research Service), p. 2.

4. *The Japanese Press*, 1983, p. 53.

5. *The Japanese Press*, 1983, p. 39.

6. Komori, "The Role of the Press in Japanese Government Decision-Making on Defense," p. 4.

7. U.S. Embassy, Tokyo, *Daily Summary of Japanese Press*, December 21, 1972, p. 17.

8. Ibid., p. 17.

9. Young C. Kim, *Japanese Journalists and Their World* (Charlottesville, Va.: University Press of Virginia), pp. 145–146.

10. Ibid., p. 144.

11. Ibid., p. 148.

12. Ibid., p. 149.

13. Ibid., p. 150.

14. Ibid., p. 152.

15. Koichi Kondō and Yoshihisa Komori, "Nihonjin kisha no kokusai kankaku" [The International Sense of Japanese Reporters], *Bungei Shunjū*, November 1983 special issue, p. 329.

16. Ibid., p. 338.

17. Ibid., p. 330.

18. U.S. Embassy, Tokyo, *Daily Summary of Japanese Press*, December 2–4, 1972, p. 1.

19. Ibid., December 1, 1970, p. 6.

20. Ibid., February 20–22, 1971, p. 1.

21. Ibid., December 1, 1972, pp. 16–17.

22. Ibid.

23. NHK Hōsō yoron chōsasho (ed.), *Zusetsu: sengo yoron shi* [A History of Postwar Public Opinion in Diagram] (Tokyo: NKH Books, 1982), p. 173.

24. Ibid., p. 173.

25. Ibid.

26. Ibid., p. 177.

27. Ibid., p. 169.

28. Ibid., p. 179.

29. U.S. Embassy, Tokyo, *Daily Summary of Japanese Press*, October 4, 1979, p. 4.

30. Ibid., October 4, 1979, pp. 1–2.

31. Ibid., November 28, 1979, p. 2.

32. Ibid., January 17, 1980, pp. 2–3.

33. Ibid., January 19–21, 1980, p. 1.

34. Ibid., January 22, 1980, p. 1.

35. Ibid., January 18, 1984, p. 3.

36. Ibid., p. 2.

37. Ibid., July 24, 1984, p. 1.

38. Ibid., September 22–25, 1984, p. 4.

39. Ibid., April 11, 1985, p. 2.

40. Ibid., August 22, 1985, p. 7. As early as August 27, 1984, *Yomiuri* had commented on the deployment of Soviet nuclear-powered cruisers in the Far East. See *Yomiuri*, August 27, 1984, p. 1. In the spring of 1984, a *Yomiuri* editorial strongly complained of Soviet military expansion in the Pacific, stating, "We cannot but express again a strong feeling of distrust toward the Soviet Union." U.S. Embassy, Tokyo, *Daily Summary of Japanese Press*, April 24, 1984, p. 1.

41. Ibid., August 22, 1985, p. 7; Sōrifu [Prime Minister's Office] (ed.), *Yoron chōsa* [A Survey of Public Opinion] (August 1985), p. 95.

42. Komori, "The Role of the Press in Japanese Government Decision-Making on Defense," p. 10.

43. Ibid., p. 11.

44. U.S. Embassy, Tokyo, *Daily Summary of Japanese Press,* July 7–9, 1984, pp. 2–3.

45. Ibid., August 22, 1984, p. 5.

46. Ibid., September 27, 1985, p. 1.

47. Komori, "The Role of the Press in Japanese Government Decision-Making on Defense," p. 11.

48. Ibid., p. 12.

49. For a latest example, see Ian Buruma, "A New Japanese Nationalism," *New York Times,* April 12, 1987, section 6. Buruma thinks Nakasone is a fascist.

50. Sōrifu, *Yoron chōsa* (August 1985), p. 95.

51. Ibid., p. 73.

52. Ibid., p. 92.

53. Ibid., p. 81.

54. Ibid., p. 95.

55. *Asahi Shimbun,* March 17, 1985, p. 1.

56. *Mainichi Shimbun,* February 25, 1987, p. 2.

5

The Defense Industry

Although Japan today ranks third in the world for annual defense spending, her defense industry is minuscule in size and importance to the economy compared to those of major NATO nations. The Yoshida strategy of shunning a large buildup of conventional forces favors continued emphasis on the economy. Accordingly, a powerful defense industry establishment—based upon interlocking interest groups with close ties to the Self-Defense Forces, government, and private industry—simply has never evolved.

Even so, Japanese critics of the defense industry contend that "while we can still talk about today's peacetime industry, there exists a latent potential for militarization."[1] They also worry that "certain industry groups and individual firms will become overly dependent on defense orders—to such an extent that they will not be able to survive without them."[2] They also point to the prospect that capital accumulation might be adversely affected by the excessive growth of the defense industry or that it will become so intertwined with U.S. strategic interests as to demand arms export in large numbers.[3] Finally, there is the fear that the defense industry is always pressing for more defense spending.[4]

None of these developments seem to have taken place in the forty years since 1945, nor have the institutional framework and procedures for defense procurement developed to substantiate the concerns of the Cassandras. To understand how defense procurement evolved after World War II and how the defense industry became so tightly regulated, we must briefly examine the origins of Japan's defense industry.

A Brief History

On September 10, 1945, the Allied occupation authorities prohibited the production of arms in Japan. But when war broke out in Korea, the United States authorized the creation of the Police Reserve in August 1950 and pressed the government to rebuild the armaments industry. In April 1952, the government created a new Security Agency (*Hoanchō*), which then amalgamated with the existing Police Reserve and finally in July 1954 became the Defense Agency.

As soon as the Korean War began, the U.S. Military Supply Agency in Japan began contracting with Japanese firms for the production of firearms, grenades, ammunition, and even vehicles. That agency spent roughly ¥52 billion in weapons contracts between 1952 and 1957, all of it to supply U.S. troops in Japan and Korea.[5] The stage was now set for the passage of the Law for the Production of Weapons (*Bukitō seizō hō*), passed on August 1, 1953 to permit the legal production of arms, ammunition, and military equipment in Japan. Between 1952 and 1956, the Defense Agency spent a total of ¥1.6 billion for the domestic production of weapons and ammunition.[6]

By 1957, there were thirty-eight private companies contracting with the agency to produce munitions and weapons.[7] Their total production value amounted to only ¥424 million in 1952 but climbed to ¥6.5 billion in 1956.[8] Yet even this rapid increase never came close to prewar production levels. For example, the ammunition output in 1954 amounted to only 7.5 percent of the output for 1938.[9]

In fact, weapons and ammunition production was a small proportion of total industrial output value in the fifties. For example, in 1955 it amounted to only 1.78 percent.[10] Weapons and ammunition production constituted roughly 4.57 percent of the value of production for the chemical industry and 8.65 percent of the machine tool industry. But as Japan's industrial production rapidly accelerated after the 1950s, the value of weapons and ammunition as a share of total industrial output never exceeded 0.50 percent even by 1984, as shown in Table 5.1.

In June 1957, the Defense Agency announced its first four-year military buildup plan, valued at ¥6.5 billion; in July 1961, the second plan called for a budget of ¥13.7 billion, followed by the third plan in February 1966 spending ¥23.5 billion. But even though the Defense Agency's procurement spending had greatly increased, its value of defense goods still was a minuscule share of total industrial value.

In fact, the value of all military equipment and weapons as a share of total industrial value was less than 0.4 percent between 1975 and 1982 (Table 5.1). The military-related supply of electronic communications equipment, vehicles, and ships also was very low, but it was very large for aircraft because Japan does not have a large civil aircraft industry. The share of total defense industry production within the total industrial output value in 1984 (0.40 percent) was far below the 1955 level of 1.78 percent.

Just as the defense industry's output has always been a minuscule share of industrial output for the past four decades, so has defense spending remained an insignificant share of the annual gross national product and of government spending. The total defense budget came to only 1.78 percent of gross national

TABLE 5.1

VALUE OF DEFENSE PRODUCTION AS A PROPORTION
OF INDUSTRIAL PRODUCTION (1975-1984)
(¥100 million; percent)

Year	Total		Ships		Aircraft		Vehicles		Weapons, Ammunition		Electronics, Communications	
	Production Value	%	Production Value	%	Production Value	%	Production Value	%	Production Value	%	Production Value	%
1975	4,051	0.37	587	1.87	1,193	86.89	95	0.09	622	99.29	753	0.76
1976	4,271	0.34	501	1.66	2,154	88.63	103	0.08	712	99.85	800	0.62
1977	4,677	0.30	769	2.48	2,240	88.37	94	0.06	715	99.80	860	0.56
1978	4,953	0.30	783	3.70	2,337	86.15	116	0.07	708	99.48	1,009	0.62
1979	5,771	0.31	1,319	8.31	2,286	85.04	133	0.07	975	99.72	1,057	0.57
1980	6,041	0.28	949	4.33	2,161	81.86	173	0.08	1,172	99.60	1,586	0.71
1981	6,097	0.27	1,289	4.83	2,210	77.76	192	0.08	1,327	99.76	1,078	0.41
1982	8,530	0.37	1,276	4.98	3,350	76.54	230	0.09	1,659	99.67	2,014	0.73
1983	9,599	0.41	1,178	4.40	3,265	77.10	272	0.10	1,975	99.80	2,909	0.92
1984	10,269	0.40	1,512	5.15	4,132	81.54	255	0.09	2,190	99.88	2,181	0.55

Source: *Confidential Draft Report* (Tokyo, 1985), pp. 39 and 41 (in Japanese).

product in 1955, fell to 1.07 percent in 1965, declined still further to 0.84 percent in 1975, and was just under 1.0 percent (0.99) in 1984 and 1985; as of 1987, it was around 1.004 percent.[11] The ratio of defense spending to all other government spending amounted to 13.61 percent in 1955, fell to 8.24 percent in 1965, slipped still lower in 1975 to 6.23 percent, and to 5.8 percent in 1984. In 1985, this figure rose slightly to 5.9 percent; it grew to 6.5 percent in 1987. In fact, the share of total defense spending in government outlays for 1987 was far lower than that for public works (11.2 percent) and education and science (8.9 percent).[12]

When Japan's defense industry is viewed in historical perspective, the spending for weapons has been minuscule in comparison to their importance for the economy in the pre-World War II period. The small defense industry that did revive in response to the Korean War never became an important component of the economy in subsequent decades. The expansion of the defense industry has been slower than the growth of industrial production over the past several decades. On balance, the defense industry accounts for a very small fraction of the industrial sector's activity.

The Structure of Defense Demand

Annual defense expenditures can be divided into two broad categories: personnel and provisions, and supplies. As for the first category, the Defense Agency contracts with private firms to supply fuel products, coal, clothing, medical supplies, food and drink, and miscellaneous items for the upkeep, replacement, and expansion of the three armed services. The production value of these supplies is less than one-fifth of total procurement spending and has remained that way over the past four decades.

The second category, supplies, consists of six subgroups, of which equipment (weapons, etc.) acquisition is the largest and covers those items demanded from and supplied by the defense industry. Table 5.2 shows the composition of defense expenditures for the period of arms expansion in 1980–1987 and underscores the importance of upgrading equipment, which as a share of defense spending rose from 50.7 to 56.1 percent. Equipment acquired included ships, aircraft, vehicles, weapons and ammunition, and electronic communications equipment.

Turning to defense procurement from domestic and foreign sources, Table 5.3 shows that in recent years about 10 percent of Japan's defense procurement has come from foreign sources.

The share of spending for equipment acquisition, one component of the defense industry's production, rose between 1977 and 1987 from 17 to 27 percent of defense spending (Table 5.2). Total defense procurement as a share of total annual defense spending remained rather constant between 1978 and 1981,

TABLE 5.2

COMPOSITION OF DEFENSE EXPENDITURES (1980-1987)
(¥ billion; percent)

	1980 Budget	1980 Distrib. Rate	1982 Budget	1982 Distrib. Rate	1984 Budget	1984 Distrib. Rate	1987 Budget	1987 Distrib. Rate
Personnel; provisions	1,100.0	49.3	1,205.0	46.6	1,309.4	44.6	543.9	43.9
Supplies:	1,130.2	50.7	1,380.0	53.4	1,625.2	55.4	1,973.6	56.1
Equipment acquisition	460.9	20.7	580.3	22.4	772.5	26.3	965.7	27.5
R & D	22.5	1.0	28.5	1.1	36.4	1.2	65.4	1.9
Facility improvement	61.4	2.8	58.6	2.3	39.3	1.3	72.2	2.0
Maintenance	314.2	14.1	408.7	15.8	454.0	15.5	499.7	14.2
Base countermeasures	232.1	10.4	268.9	10.4	285.5	9.7	439.9	9.4
Other	39.2	1.8	35.8	1.4	37.5	1.3	40.7	1.1
TOTAL	2,230.2	100.0	2,568.1	100.0	2,934.6	100.0	40.7	100.0

Notes: 1. Equipment acquisition expenditures include those for weapons, aircraft, and vessels.
2. Maintenance expenditures include those for housing, clothing, and training.
3. The component ratio of the budget is below 100 percent because fractions of breakdown figures are rounded.

Source: *Defense of Japan, 1984*, p. 264; *Defense of Japan, 1987*, p. 305. Figures are based on original budget.

TABLE 5.3

SOURCES OF EQUIPMENT PROCUREMENT (1950-1985)

(¥ million)

	Domestic Procurement (A)	Commercial Imports (B)	Foreign Military Sales (C)	Military Assistance Program (D)	Total (E)	Ratio of Domestic Procurement (%) (A/E)
1950-1957	2,415	95	25	3,569	6,104	39.6
1st Defense Buildup Plan (1958-1960)	2,789	109	168	1,405	4,471	62.4
1961	702	63	60	261	1,086	64.6
2nd Defense Buildup Plan (1962-1966)	5,781	424	382	497	7,084	81.6
3rd Defense Buildup Plan (1967-1971)	12,829	662	478	33	14,002	91.6
4th Defense Buildup Plan (1972-1976)	21,588	1,001	617	0	23,206	93.0
1977	5,846	222	194	0	6,261	93.4
1978	7,126	209	1,014	0	8,349	85.4
1979	7,373	394	885	0	8,652	85.2
1980	10,506	567	801	0	11,875	88.5
1981	8,158	604	1,386	0	10,130	80.5
1982	12,425	618	978	0	14,020	88.6
1983	12,673	598	758	0	14,029	90.3
1984	12,791	787	528	0	14,107	90.7
1985	13,417	636	707	0	14,760	90.9

Source: *Defense of Japan, 1985*, p. 297 and JDA (for 1984); and *Defense of Japan, 1987*, p. 310.

but then jumped by 21 percent in 1982, only to decline in 1985, the last year data were available. Other spending items, such as supporting U.S. base facilities, also account for the 1981–1982 rise in procurement spending. Finally, spending for defense procurement greatly exceeded the funds spent on the defense industry, because it includes spending for research and development, facility improvements, maintenance, base countermeasures, and so on (see Table 5.1).

In 1982, Japan purchased under licensed contracts with the United States around $567 million worth of defense equipment, an amount enough to rank Japan as second among the top ten countries that have military contracts with the United States.[13] Similarly, Japan produced under contracts with Italy and Britain several hundred million dollars worth of aircraft equipment, guided missiles, and parts for weapons[14] (Table 5.3, Column C). If we ignore the military equipment that is imported and produced under foreign licenses, the share of domestic military procurement for equipment has remained well over 80 percent, with only minor fluctuations above that level occurring since 1961[15] (Table 5.3, last column).

The Structure of the Defense Industry

Each year, the Defense Agency contracts with private firms on a bidding basis to produce equipment, weapons, and supplies. If we examine only equipment and weapons, in 1983 twenty private enterprises supplied 73.5 percent of all procurement spending from the government (Table 5.4).

Three large firms accounted for roughly two-fifths of all defense contracts, because defense production is dispersed among many firms. The proportion of defense production value out of each firm's total sales is less than 17 percent. Except for the Japan Steelworks, the remaining firms produce less than 10 percent of their total output for the Defense Agency. In this regard, conditions in Japan are very different from those in the United States. Of the top fifteen U.S. defense contractors, ten companies depend on defense contracts for more than 20 percent of their total sales (Table 5.5). In short, these U.S. companies are more dependent upon defense production than even the three Japanese firms with the largest defense contracts.

Have the same top ten or twenty Japanese companies that engaged in defense contracts in the 1950s retained their same ranking in the early 1980s? Such stability could produce powerful lobbying interests that would try to influence government defense spending. When we compare the top twenty Japanese defense contractors in Table 5.6 with those of the early 1980s (Table 5.4), we find that only Steel Works, Mitsubishi Heavy Industries, and Kawasaki Shipbuilding have survived, while the others have bowed out of defense contracts or amalgamated with other companies.

Even though nearly three-quarters of all defense contracts in 1983 were made with only twenty large corporations, these corporations then subcontracted much

TABLE 5.4

THE TOP 20 JAPANESE DEFENSE CONTRACTORS (FY 1983)

Rank	Company	Defense Contracts (¥ million)	Share in Total Defense Contracts (%)	Ratio of Each Firm's Sales (%)
1	Mitsubishi Heavy Industries	205,907	18.5	10.8
2	Nippon Electric	124,532	11.2	8.5
3	Kawasaki Heavy Industries	113,764	10.2	16.9
4	Ishikawajima-Harima Heavy Industries	84,037	7.6	9.2
5	Mitsubishi Electric Corp.	73,274	6.6	4.6
6	Toshiba Corp.	49,197	4.4	2.4
7	Japan Steel Works	22,977	2.1	17.6
8	Nippon Oil	17,162	1.5	0.5
9	Fuji Heavy Industries	16,920	1.5	2.8
10	Komatsu	14,523	1.3	2.4
11	Mitsubishi Precision	12,151	1.1	—
12	Maruzen Oil	10,940	1.0	0.7
13	Hitachi Zosen Corp.	10,580	1.0	2.6
14	Fujitsu	10,230	0.9	1.0
15	Daikin Industries	9,736	0.9	6.0
16	Nissho Iwai Corp.	8,849	0.8	0.1
17	Daikyo Oil Corp.	8,508	0.8	0.7
18	Kyodo Oil	8,193	0.7	—
19	Idemitsu Kosan Co.	7,914	0.7	0.3
20	Oki Electric Industry	7,537	0.7	2.5
TOTAL		816,930	73.5	

Source: Defense Production Committee, Keidanren, *Defense Production in Japan*, Table 2.

TABLE 5.5

THE TOP 15 U.S. DEFENSE CONTRACTORS (FY 1983)

Rank	Company	Defense Contracts ($ million)	Share in Total Defense Contracts (%)	Ratio of Each Firm's Sales (%)
1	General Dynamics Corp.	6,818	5.32	80
2	McDonnel Douglas Corp.	6,143	4.79	70-80
3	Rockwell International Corp.	4,545	3.54	50
4	General Electric Co.	4,518	3.52	15
5	Boeing Co.	4,423	3.45	40
6	Lockheed Corp.	4,006	3.12	60
7	United Technologies Corp.	3,867	3.02	20-30
8	Tenneco, Inc. (Newport News Shipbld. & Dry Dock)	3,762	2.93	—
9	Hughes Aircraft	3,240	2.53	—
10	Raytheon Co.	2,728	2.13	40-50
11	Grumman Corp.	2,298	1.79	90
12	Martin Marietta Corp.	2,272	1.77	50-60
13	Litton	2,169	1.69	40
14	Westinghouse Electric Corp.	1,778	1.39	10-20
15	IBM	1,421	1.11	3
TOTAL		128,242	100.00	—

Source: *Aviation Week & Space Technology*, April 23, 1984.

TABLE 5.6

THE TOP 20 JAPANESE DEFENSE CONTRACTORS (EARLY 1950s)
(U.S.$)

Rank	Company	Contracts
1	Fuji Automobile	37,159,567
2	Japan Steel Works	18,702,862
3	Mitsubishi Heavy Industries	17,113,784
4	Victor Automobiles	8,237,308
5	Shōwa Aircraft	8,215,245
6	Japan Steel	4,375,289
7	New Mitsubishi Heavy Industry	4,048,524
8	Hino Diesel	3,386,675
9	Kawasaki Shipping Industries	2,946,455
10	Japan Steel Construction	1,638,892
11	Japan Shipbuilding	1,424,319
12	Uraga Docks	1,350,279
13	Tokyo-Yokohama Industry	1,297,644
14	Yamamoto Machine Works	883,907
15	Kawa Minami Works	717,593
16	Kyōhama Automobile	662,460
17	Kanewa Docks	547,500
18	Yokohama Shipbuilding	491,853
19	Toyota Auto Sales	463,542
20	Sasebo Shipbuilding	432,483

Source: Akagi Shōichi, *Nihon bōei sangyō,* [Japan's
Defense Industry] (Tokyo: Sanichi Shobo, 1969),
p. 50.

of that work to other firms, so that as many as 800 companies are actually involved in producing most defense equipment.[16] In the last decade, the overall number of subcontracting enterprises has remained rather constant. In the United States, the number of subcontracting firms that produce defense goods amounts to as many as 25,000 to 30,000, and in West Germany the figure is around 2,000. Although many small and medium-size enterprises are engaged in Japan's defense production, only firms capitalized at over U.S.$80 million produced around 80 percent of all defense production.[17] In 1966, around 433,000 people were employed in defense-related industry. Japan's total work force came to 48.7 million people, of whom roughly one-third (15.5 million) were employed in the secondary sector (mining, construction, and manufacturing). The defense industry's share of secondary manufacturing employment came to 2.7 percent.

However, it is likely that most personnel straddled defense and civilian contracts within their respective firms, since few firms in Japan can survive on defense contracts alone.

Of the total number employed in the defense industry, only 3.2 percent were researchers, and their number was largest in the electronic communications sector. Although we lack data for the mid-1980s, if we extrapolate the annual manpower growth rate (3 percent) in the four sectors of the defense industry for the period 1962–1966, we arrive at a figure of 581,160. In 1980, total employment in the secondary sector came to 18.7 million, so that the defense industry's estimated share in this sector's labor force amounted to 3.1 percent. Even if we include the labor force employed in defense-ordered shipbuilding, it is unlikely that the industry's share of the secondary sector's employment exceeded 5.0 percent in the 1980s. Even by 1988, very few resources in the economy were utilized solely for defense procurement.

As for the distribution of capital equipment, experimental equipment, and so on throughout the defense industrial sector, the largest concentration of machines was in the electronic communications sector, followed by aircraft, weapons, and vehicles. The highest share of experimental equipment was also in the electronic communications sector.

From the above discussion, the term "defense industry" must be used with caution in Japan's case, since very few firms could survive on defense contracts alone. For nearly all firms, defense contracts constitute only a small, sideline production dwarfed by civilian production. Moreover, the firms that dominated the defense industry during the 1950s did not do so in the 1980s. In the early 1980s, none of the top twenty firms greatly depended upon their defense contracts as a main source of their sales. Even the main equipment items produced under license from foreign firms have not been concentrated in the hands of a few powerful domestic firms, but are widely distributed among the top twenty firms.[18]

The Defense Procurement System

All major sectors of the Japanese government play a consultative and intervening role in the military procurement system. The Defense Agency is tremendously circumscribed, controlled, and regulated by different branches of government. In fact, procurement planning is a tedious process involving many branches of government, and all requests are carefully reviewed at every step of the way.[19]

All plans and requests for military procurement originate in the Defense Agency's staff offices of the Ground, Maritime, and Air Defense Forces. In these three staff offices, an echelon of military experts draws up annual procurement requests. In each of these staff offices, planning, logistics, and technology departments study trends in the defense industry in Japan, as well as in foreign countries. They occasionally send experts to NATO and to the U.S. Department of Defense to observe the testing and use of new weapons and equipment. Based on such detailed investigations, the three departments formulate their plans and requests for the staff offices, taking care to make accurate cost estimates and provide justification for all new weapons and equipment. The three staff offices then send their requests to three separate Defense Agency bureaus: Defense, Equipment, and Finance.

The Defense Bureau examines all requests from the standpoint of long-term defense planning. The Equipment Bureau examines all technical, efficiency, and cost aspects of equipment requests. It also supervises a Technology Institute that cooperates with private enterprises and studies trends in military research and development. The Equipment Bureau, whose director by custom is on temporary loan from the Ministry of International Trade and Industry (MITI), is especially well informed of the technical and industrial implications of any procurement plan that comes from staff offices. This bureau must decide whether new equipment should be imported, acquired through licensed production, or produced at home. The Finance Bureau then examines all procurement requests with a keen eye to their costs, previous cost overruns, and its knowledge of current budgetary restraints within the Defense Agency.

Senior representatives of all three bureaus convene, discuss, and eventually agree upon a procurement plan. Meanwhile, informal meetings have taken place within the Defense Agency among the Ground, Maritime, and Air Self-Defense Forces' staff offices and the three bureaus. These meetings have dealt with issues on a case-by-case basis so that when the three bureaus reach a final agreement a consensus on the new procurement plan has also been reached within the Defense Agency. Such discussions by the staff offices and bureaus usually takes between six and nine months to reach a final agreement for each fiscal year.

The Defense Agency then submits the new procurement plan immediately to MITI and the Ministry of Finance, which review the plan. Finance takes a tough attitude toward all budget requests and reviews them within the context of all government outlays in the forthcoming budget. The ministry strictly adhered to the general guideline of keeping military expenditures under 1 percent of gross national product until 1987. For example, a proposal for new equipment in 1984 called for establishing the Patriot system of surface-to-air missiles, but the ministry rejected it as too expensive.

The relevant departments in MITI, meanwhile, also review the new procurement plan from many perspectives. MITI pays close attention to the prospective recipients of Defense Agency contracts and carefully reviews each, especially where licensing is involved, to determine its likely impact upon industrial development. MITI also evaluates Defense Agency recommendations for foreign-licensed production and commercial import.

After the Defense Agency's new defense plan has been studied, modified, and finally approved by MITI and the Ministry of Finance, it is sent to the National

Defense Council (*Kokubō kaigi*). This council consists of the deputy prime minister, foreign minister, finance minister, Defense Agency director, and the director of the Economic Planning Agency. A number of working-level meetings are held before the council carefully reviews and approves the new defense plan before sending it to the prime minister's office for cabinet approval.

While the National Defense Council reviews the Defense Agency's plan, its members have already consulted with a group of key LDP leaders (for example, those on the LDP Defense Committee) and elicited their approval. In this way the LDP leadership can inform its members in the Diet and mobilize support for the defense plan when it comes before the budget committees and both houses of the Diet. After all government agencies have checked and rechecked the new defense plan and finally approved it, the Diet must then vote its approval.

Even at the inception of the new defense procurement plan in the Defense Agency, various bureaus are already consulting with the organ that represents Japanese manufacturers, Keidanren. Keidanren's defense production committees and the representatives of leading corporations obtain information about the new equipment, weapons, and so on that might ultimately be contracted out for production by private industry.

Meanwhile, the Defense Agency might ask key corporations like Kawasaki, Fuji, or Mitsubishi to conduct research to determine whether certain equipment or weapons can be efficiently produced. The Defense Agency already knows a great deal about the industrial corporations to which it may eventually let contracts. When the Defense Agency initially consulted MITI on the new defense procurement plan, both bureaucracies considered which companies might best produce the equipment and weapons projected in the defense plan. Even before the Diet has approved the new procurement plan, there is general understanding within MITI and Defense as to which firms will be considered for bids and final award of contracts. Yet final bidding for contracts is not a foregone conclusion; the number of prospective bidders has simply been reduced. After the Diet has approved the new defense procurement plan, the Defense Agency solicits bidding. MITI never intervenes any further. Bids are reviewed by the Center for Quality Control within the Defense Agency. Upon awarding a contract, the Defense Agency informs the enterprise of the contract requirements, and the contractor has the right of first refusal if it cannot meet the contract's standards and stipulations.

Laws Regulating the Defense Agency's Procurement

The above process has been institutionalized and in place since the early 1950s. Two important laws enable the government to control the Defense Agency: the Law for Enterprises Manufacturing Aircraft, passed July 16, 1952, and the Law for Manufacturing Weapons and Munitions, passed August 1, 1953.[20] These statutes allow MITI to regulate and control the manufacturing of all aircraft and parts, weapons, and munitions in order to control defense procurement.

Both laws require private firms to provide detailed information about location, ownership, type of technology used, capitalization, and more to MITI. The firms also must submit complete plans of their defense projects and describe all equipment to be used, costs, technology, and so on. MITI makes a full review of all applications and approves or rejects them. If an enterprise fails to begin a project within a year, MITI can revoke its permission retroactively. MITI also can send inspectors to aircraft manufacturers and review their current production procedures and more. It is significant that this hair-splitting scrutiny of defense production was institutionalized in the 1960s, when the ruling LDP gave in to pacific pressures in the Diet.

Research and Development in the Defense Industry

One indicator to evaluate defense industry activity is how much defense spending goes to research and development (R & D). Modern states allocating a lot of spending for military R & D usually innovate and have large defense budgets.

If we compare Japan's defense R & D spending with that of other countries, both in absolute level and as a share of government defense spending, Japan is not a major innovator in defense production. Defense R & D spending in Japan in 1984 came to only 1.49 percent of defense expenditures, or ¥43.8 billion. This compares to 11.0 percent, or ¥6,267 billion, for the United States; 12.4 percent, or ¥770.8 billion, for the United Kingdom; 4.1 percent, or ¥188.3 billion, for West Germany; and 12.1 percent, or ¥550.4 billion, for France.[21] Japan not only spent less on R & D, but it spent a smaller share of its total defense spending than did other countries.

When a nation increases defense spending and makes greater investment in capital stock for defense production, R & D spending for defense rises. This certainly was true for Europe and the United States, but not for Japan. Between 1973 and 1985, Japan's defense expenditures rose 3.3 times. Capital expenditures for the same period rose 3.3 times, and spending for new military equipment and so on rose 3.4 times. But when we relate defense R & D to capital spending between 1973 and 1985, the ratio was 29.8 percent in 1973 and 29.2 percent in 1985—virtually no change.[22] In fact, that ratio declined during the late 1970s, and only rose gradually in the early 1980s, to reach the same level in 1985 as in 1973. Similarly, defense R & D spending as a share of defense expenditures was 1.30 percent in 1973, 0.97 percent in 1979, 1.1 percent in 1982, and 1.61 percent in 1985, or virtually unchanged.

Some Keidanren experts contend that Japan's defense industry primarily benefits from technological progress in civilian industries rather than from direct defense R & D. According to Masudo Kinya, "Instead of the civilian industry receiving a spinoff from the military, it is the other way around here."[23]

The government also kept unit costs for weapons and equipment from rising too rapidly and prevented excessive cost overruns when contracting with private firms. This is quite an achievement because of the high rate of obsolescence associated with long-term acquisition of defense weapons and equipment. Because public opinion and government policy are adamantly opposed to any export of arms and munitions, the government cannot sell them abroad, even secondhand. The Defense Agency must scrap weapons and equipment as they become obsolete.

In a rare show of unity, Japan's aircraft and arms manufacturers recently lobbied for the home development of a new generation of jet fighter (the FSX), a request that collided with the U.S. Pentagon's desire to sell fighters to Japan. Yet this FSX lobby had no interest in selling the product abroad. Its immediate interest was to maintain and upgrade the engineering staff for airframe design; autonomous engine development was not in the plan because it was considered too costly. Japan's interest in the Strategic Defense Initiative, or "Star Wars," is of a similar nature—Japan simply wants to keep up with the latest technological development having a potential for military and civilian uses.

The Ground Self-Defense Force's manpower ceiling now stands at 180,000, as stipulated in 1954. But that armed service began embarking on new R & D in 1983 for ship-based antisubmarine helicopters to supersede those already in service (HSS-28). For the navy, surface-to-ship missiles are being developed. New bombs with guidance systems also are being developed for the same purpose. The Defense Agency is also encouraging R & D for producing a device to be installed on minesweepers to sweep moored mines that have been placed at any depth. These and other new weapon systems and equipment have been slated for development in the eighties.

The relationship between the defense industry and the national economy is very different from that of the pre-World War II period. The "defense industry" is a sideline function of Japan's commercial production. Not only does the defense industry use few resources, but its influence upon the economy is minuscule. Furthermore, little concentration of economic power among firms exists in the defense industry; no powerful interest groups can influence national defense policy and spending. Japan's industrial giants cannot export defense weapons and equipment abroad, and they must produce these at higher unit cost for domestic use only. Japan's defense industry continues to confound the "merchant of death" alarmists.

Notes

1. Kazuo Tomiyama, *Nihon no bōei sangyō* [Japan's Defense Industry] (Tokyo: Toyo Keizai Shimpōsha, 1979), p. 15.

2. Kazuo Tomiyama, "Weapons Manufacturers Continue to Grow," *Japan Quarterly*, July/September 1982, p. 344.

3. Ibid., pp. 344–345.

4. Ibid., p. 345.

5. *Nihon heiki kōgyōkai* [Japanese Military Weapons Industry Association], *Buki seisan kōzō chōsa* [A Survey of the Structure of Weapons Production], in *Kikai kōgyō kiso chōsa* [Basic Survey of the Machine Industry], no. 4, pp. 98–99.

6. Ibid.

7. Ibid., p. 100.

8. Ibid., pp. 105–107 for a list of the firms allowed to produce weapons and ammunition under the August 1952 law legalizing military ordnance production.

9. Ibid., p. 104 for such estimates by the Nihon keiki kōgyōkai.

10. Obtained from *Confidential Draft Report, 1985* (p. 41), given to Ramon H. Myers by a government official in April 1985.

11. The Defense Agency, *Defense of Japan, 1985* (Tokyo: Japan Times, 1986), p. 302.

12. The Defense Agency, *Defense of Japan, 1987* (Tokyo: Japan Times, 1987), p. 148.

13. See Table 6 in Defense Production Committee, Keidanren, *Defense Production in Japan* (Tokyo, 1985), supplied to Ramon H. Myers in April 1985.

14. Ibid., Table 5.

15. Defense Production Committee, Keidanren, *Statistical Tables*, April 1985, Table 7. See column 6 of that table.

16. Ibid., p. 56.

17. *Confidential Draft Report, 1985*, p. 53.

18. *Defense Production in Japan*, Table 5.

19. This section is based on interviews with officials of MITI and the Defense Agency in 1985.

20. See Ryūichi Hirano, Ichirō Ogawa, Ichirō Kato, Akira Mikazuki (compilers), *Roppō zensho* (Tokyo: Yūhikaku, 1984), vol. I, pp. 1134–1135 for Bukitō seizōhō, and vol. II, pp. 3382–3383 for Kōkuki seizō kigyōhō.

21. *Defense Production in Japan*, Table 7. The conversion rates used were: US$1 = ¥238; £1 = ¥366; DM1 = ¥95; and FFr1 = ¥32.

22. Ibid., Table 8.

23. "Arms Industry Booming Despite Ban," *Japan Times Weekly*, October 13, 1984, p. 4.

6

The Armed Services

Since 1945 there has been an across-the-board agreement among the Japanese people that two major factors—one international and the other domestic, were responsible for the disastrous consequences of World War II. The international factor was the dissolution of the Anglo-Japanese alliance at the Washington Conference in 1921. The other was the Meiji Constitution, which provided for direct command of the military by the Emperor rather than by the Diet. Ironically, the intention behind this arrangement was to prevent the politicization of the armed forces. While the Meiji oligarchs actually ruled the state in the name of the emperor, they kept both the Diet and the military under control. With the passing of the oligarchs from the scene by the early 1920s, the government became hydra-headed, with the Diet going one way and the military another. Long before MacArthur's arrival, there was an incipient movement to amend the constitution to ensure civilian supremacy, but to no avail.[1] Japan's defeat reinforced popular hope for the principle of civilian supremacy. From the constitutional revisionists to the Socialists, no one in Japan questions this principle.

The Command Structure

The difficulty with civilian control since 1945 has rather been that the concept was interpreted in an excessively antimilitary fashion. The joint efforts of MacArthur and Yoshida have left a lasting legacy to the institutions of the Japanese military. When the Korean War broke out and rearmament became imperative, MacArthur had to circumvent the constitution by ordering the Police Reserve—the forerunner of today's Self-Defense Forces—into being. He did so by executive decree rather than through legislation. These facts together cast a pall of illegitimacy on the new army.[2] Prime Minister Yoshida seized on this order to entrust the founding of the army to the police establishment rather than to the former officers of the Imperial Army and Navy. Early directors of the Defense Agency were police officials who hailed from the prewar Interior Ministry, by far the most elite bureaucracy in its time. Until quite recently, some of the most important posts in the civilian bureaucracy at the Defense Agency were filled by former police officials. Primarily, civilian control came to mean subordination of the three uniformed services to the civilian bureaucracy in the Defense Agency.

But here again the Americans reinforced what the Japanese were doing. In supervising the founding of the Police Reserve, the occupation authority devised and laid down a system of civilian control that was very different from that in the U.S. Department of Defense. To put the American system simply, there are two parallel hierarchies, one made up of the armed services and the other of civilian administrators in the Defense Department. The division of labor is between military operation and military administration. The two hierarchies come together in the office of the secretary of defense, a cabinet officer.

This was not the system decreed by Lt. Gen. Lemuel C. Sheperd, who was acting in the capacity of chief of the Military Advisory and Assistance Group vis-à-vis the Police Reserve. Instead, he subordinated the military hierarchy to the civilian hierarchy before subordinating the latter to the elected cabinet official who corresponded to America's secretary of defense. The Japanese were told that the Police Reserve headquarters should be staffed by civilian officials with a controlling voice in all major policies—military as well as administrative. To greatly simplify the matter, one could say that the civilian administrators were to function collectively as a counterpart of the U.S. defense secretary. Therefore, it would have been straightforward if the military did not have any direct input to the director of defense. But the Japanese were told that the uniformed officers were also to have a place at the headquarters as staff to the director. Such a relationship had no counterpart in Japanese organizational lore, civilian or military. Nor was the relationship ever explained to the satisfaction of the Japanese. They decided to let a satisfactory arrangement evolve out of trial and error.[3]

Two legislative acts passed in 1954 laid down the framework of the Defense Agency and the Self-Defense Forces, and they reaffirmed the basic scheme of the founders. At the Defense Agency, all the civilian offices (the Secretariat, the bureaus of Defense, Personnel, Budget, Equipment, and Training) were given the status of inner bureau (*naikyoku*). Until then, no one who served in uniform could transfer to the inner bureau. Though this was changed in 1954, no important civilian job has been given to a military officer since. The Joint Staff Council (JSC), modeled after the Joint Chiefs of Staff, was authorized. But the JSC, the three chiefs of staff, and the services were designated outer bureau (*gaikyoku*). The distinction, an old one in Japanese civil service, separates pure administration-supervision from the service or production function. This distinction is justified on the grounds that an inner bureau has much more intense administrative contact with the director of the Defense Agency, not that an inner bureau confines itself to pure administration.[4]

The 1954 acts also authorized a system of councilors—up to eight in number—who collectively function as the highest policy-making staff to advise and assist the director. The chiefs of Secretariat and the five bureaus are concurrently councilors.[5] This creates room for a councilor or two without a line responsibility, who could devote his time to major policy-making. So far, the post of full-time councilor has been given to a Foreign Ministry transferee.

The constitution puts the supreme political power in the Diet and its committee, the cabinet. Furthermore, it stipulates—strangely enough for a no-war constitution—that cabinet ministers be civilians. The prime minister has the highest authority over the Defense Agency, but he is not the commander-in-chief. The service chiefs and the JSC chairman advise the director of defense, but not the prime minister. In operational matters, the line of command goes from the Defense Agency director, to the chiefs of staff of the respective services, and then down to the services. The JSC does not have a line responsibility; the chairman of JSC has a role in advising the director, and the JSC chairman's decision must be based on a unanimous vote of the JSC.[6] It was the collective pressure of the inner bureau that kept the JSC chairman a mere figurehead, a pressure that continues to date.

Civilian control came to mean control of the military by the inner bureau, made up of career civil servants. Of course, they are in turn accountable to the director of defense, who is in turn answerable to the Diet. But the Diet did not function until recently the way parliamentary bodies in other democracies do. With the major opposition party bent on abolishing the military altogether, the Diet became the arena of sterile dispute on the legality of armed forces. Substantive military policy was seldom debated. This situation did not change until after the fall of Saigon. Even today the opposition parties keep a distance from the security affairs, and the Diet's control of the military actually means LDP control.[7]

Partly because of Prime Minister Yoshida's attitude, the Defense Agency itself was accorded a less-than-equal status among the central ministries. It is an agency in the prime minister's office, and major appointments in the Defense Agency civilian bureaucracy are customarily given to transferees from other ministries, including the police agency. This does not mean that the transferees practice bureaucratic turf wars within the Defense Agency; their impact on Defense is much more subtle and sometimes quite desirable. But in the case of the Foreign Ministry, there is definitely an organizational will to dominate substantive policy in national security. In weapons acquisition and transfer of military technology, MITI plays an important role, as detailed in Chapter 5. The domination of the Defense Agency by other ministries makes it difficult for the agency to recruit good civilian officials.

In 1956, the National Defense Council (NDC) was established by law in the cabinet with the hope that it would function in much the same way that the National Security Council in the White House does. It is attended by the prime minister; ministers of Foreign Affairs, Finance, Economic Planning; the Defense Agency director; and such a minister of state as the prime minister deems fit. Since the founding, the NDC has taken part in the statutory advisory role over all major national security decisions. The NDC must also be consulted when the prime minister decides to mobilize the military.

The primary concern of the Defense Agency during the long winter of neglect (which lasted until 1978) was to appease the anti-war Diet and the media. More than one director lost his job because of a slip of the tongue. The tyranny of the media is tapering off. But with security issues becoming more important since 1978, defects in Japan's security arrangement began to cry out for attention. It fell to military officers to blow the whistle. The Guideline for Japan-U.S. Defense Cooperation agreed upon between U.S. Defense Secretary James Schlesinger and M. Sakata, his Japanese counterpart, authorized mutual consultation, joint planning, and exercises by U.S. and Japanese forces. The Pentagon and CINCPAC (Commander-in-Chief, Pacific) also became a strong defense lobby in Japan. Since 1978 the Diet has begun to interest itself in substantive security issues. The LDP's defense lobby came into existence. A special committee, not yet a standing committee, on defense was created in both houses of the Diet in 1984. All these factors created a renewed interest in the question of civilian control.

General Hiroomi Kurisu, chairman of the JSC and the highest-ranking officer in 1978, joined the Self-Defense Forces at the time of its founding and stayed on, spurning chances of promotion within another ministry. During the defense debate in 1978 he decided to buck the organization and go public in an attempt to right some of the defects in Japan's defense establishment. Though he was dismissed, he performed a valuable role in public debate. His dissatisfaction concerned the procedure of "civilian control" as then practiced, in which the voice of the professional military was sidetracked by the bureaucratic civilians and did not reach the true "civilians" in the Diet or the prime minister.

The military professionals complained of being restricted by encrusted bureaucratic rules that frustrated them in the performance of their duties.[8] As chairman of the JSC, Kurisu had the statutory duty of intelligence collection, but he was barred from briefing the director. That was done by the inner bureau, which resisted revising the threat estimate in the Defense White Papers of 1977 and 1978. By custom, the military was barred from testifying before the Diet, and neither the JSC chairman nor the service chiefs had ever been consulted by the prime minister.

General Kurisu's remarks clearly implied a different organization chart for civilian control. For him, civilian control meant, first and foremost, political control by the Diet. It did not mean control of the military by the inner bureau. "It is a silly thesis to say that military operations fall under military administration," he said.[9] He was advocating the exact parallel of the U.S. Department of Defense. There is much to be said for this simply in terms of organization tables. However, we must reckon with two facts. One is that, given the weight of the postwar tradition, such a change would involve a major bureaucratic fight, which could undermine the common interest of the Defense Agency as a whole. The other has to do with the collective profile of the Defense Agency director, who would single-handedly control the military under the proposed scheme. The director's job usually goes to a young member of the Diet as his first cabinet appointment, from whence he ascends to elite ministries. Moreover, no director in the last twenty years has served more than one year at a stretch because of frequent cabinet shuffles. This is a far cry from the case of, say, Caspar Weinberger, who served for seven years at the Pentagon.

A major reorganization of the Defense Agency and its elevation to the ministry status are desirable over the long haul, but pending that, a less drastic way to ensure a hearing for the military is possible. That is to elevate the JSC chairman from a figurehead role to a place in the chain of command by subordinating service chiefs to the chairman. The Self-Defense Forces are barred from projecting power abroad, and their military operations are confined to an area no larger than the state of Montana. Their military resources, too, are strictly limited. Close cooperation and coordination of the three services is vital. But in the past each service tended to go off on its own with an American counterpart but without regard to the other services. The military needs an office that can represent its collective voice to the inner bureau, the Diet, and the public. No one can handle this task but the JSC chairman. A revision of the 1954 statute on this point seems overdue.[10]

There are other issues in civilian control. Each house of the Diet needs a standing committee on defense instead of a special committee. Uniformed officers should be allowed to testify before Diet committees. The JSC chairman's intelligence briefing for the Defense director has been instituted. Prime Minister Nakasone consulted JSC members regularly on matters having to do with their professional competence. This should be expanded and institutionalized.

The Modernization of the Self-Defense Forces

By 1988, the Self-Defense Forces had an authorized force of well over a quarter-million personnel. The Ground Self-Defense Forces, the largest of the three, had an authorized force of 180,000 men, made up of twelve divisions and seven specialized brigades such as armor, artillery, airborne, and helicopters.[11] The authorized level was 90 percent filled, and this figure did not change in the next decade. The Air Self-Defense Forces, the next service in size, had an authorized strength of 47,000 men, comprising twenty-eight air control and warning units, ten squadrons of interceptors, three squadrons of ground support fighters, one squadron of reconnaissance, three squadrons of air transport, and six batteries of high-altitude ground-to-air missiles. The Maritime Self-Defense

Force, with 45,500 men, had fifty-two destroyer-escorts, fourteen diesel-powered submarines, eighty fixed-wing aircraft, and seventy-one helicopters.

What will the Self-Defense Forces look like by 1990, when the goals of the military buildup set in the revised National Defense Program Outline are fulfilled? Japan will have acquired 187 fighter aircraft in ten squadrons, of which seven will have F-15s and three will have improved F-4 Phantoms. Twelve E-2C early warning aircraft will be operational and will be augmented by AWACS. As for air and sea defense, six batteries of ground-to-air missile forces will have Patriot missiles to replace the current Nikes. Five batteries of Hawk ground-to-air missile forces will also receive improved weapons. On the sea, Japan will acquire sixty-two frigates and sixteen conventional submarines. The first Aegis missile frigate will join this fleet shortly. Many of these ships will be new. One hundred fixed-wing antisubmarine aircraft, of which ninety-four will be P3-C Orions, will be operational. Such a huge fleet could terrorize Soviet submarines. For coastline defense, Japan will have three batteries of shore-to-ship missiles, five squadrons of antitank helicopters (AH-1s), thirty-two transport helicopters (CH-47s) for greater mobility, and three squadrons of ground support fighter-bombers. The Ground Self-Defense Force will have 1,210 tanks, 949 armored personnel carriers, and improved firepower.

For an improvement in surveillance of Soviet movements in Siberia and Sakhalin, Japan will soon acquire the over-the-horizon radar. The Self-Defense Forces will also either acquire a link-up with a U.S. communications satellite network or have one of their own that will feed into the U.S. network. The total cost of this five-year plan, expressed in 1980 prices, will be $123 billion (at $1.00 per ¥150).

The SDFs and U.S. Military Cooperation

A new development since the late 1970s has been closer cooperation between the Self-Defense Forces and U.S. armed forces. This began with a meeting of the defense chiefs of the two countries after the fall of Saigon. In August 1983, Defense Agency Director Tanikawa Kazuo met with Secretary of Defense Caspar W. Weinberger, and they agreed that closer cooperation between the two allies was necessary to cope with the Soviet Union's recently expanded military power. Tanikawa expressed his country's hope that the negotiations between Washington and Moscow to eliminate intermediate-range nuclear forces would encompass SS-20 missiles deployed worldwide, not only those in Europe. The United States appreciated Japan's interests but insisted that Japan make more efforts to upgrade its defense. Tanikawa responded that Japan had been doing this since the late 1970s while the government elicited popular support for these new efforts. The United States wanted to deploy F-16 fighters to the Misawa Air Base in northern Japan, and Japan agreed. The United States also asked for cooperation in landing practice for carrier-

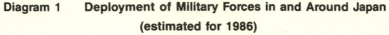

Diagram 1 Deployment of Military Forces in and Around Japan (estimated for 1986)

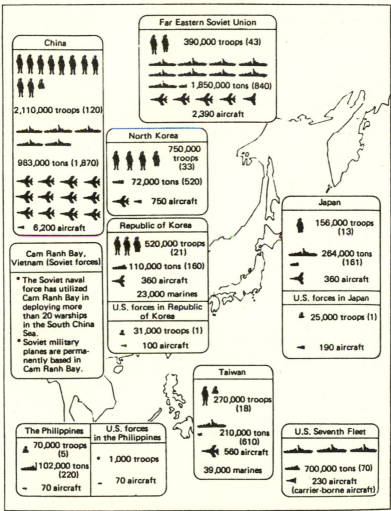

Notes:

1. Figures for Japan show actual strength as of the end of fiscal 1986.

2. The number of U.S. forces personnel stationed in various countries in the total of army personnel and marines.

3. Soviet forces at Cam Ranh Bay are a part of the Soviet forces in the Far East.

4. Combat aircraft in the Far Eastern Soviet Union, China and those maintained by U.S. forces stationed in various countries include naval and marine aircraft.

5. Figures in the parentheses indicate the number of army divisions or vessels.

borne aircraft, which was granted. In meetings such as these it was decided by mid-1984 that the chief of staff of U.S. forces in Japan and counselors at the U.S. embassy should meet with top-ranking Japanese officials at least once every few weeks to consult on how to implement the Status of Forces Agreement, which would cover a wide range of topics relevant to the alliance.

As of spring 1984, there were about 45,700 U.S. military forces in Japan, headquarted at Yokota Air Base in Tokyo. The commander of these forces met regularly with the Defense Agency and other Japanese ministries and agencies to discuss matters of joint military cooperation. U.S. Army forces are represented by a headquarters unit at Camp Zama in Kanagawa Prefecture. U.S. Navy forces are at Yokosuka in the same prefecture, and the U.S. Marine Corps has an amphibious force headquartered at Camp Courtney on Okinawa. The U.S. Fifth Air Force deploys one tactical fighter wing at Kadena Air Base on Okinawa and one tactical airlift group at Yokota Air Base.

The Ground Self-Defense Force began operating with U.S. forces by undertaking communications training and command post exercises in 1981. The Maritime Self-Defense Force had staged training exercises with U.S. forces in Japan, focusing on antisubmarine and minesweeping exercises, as early as 1955.[12] In June 1984, a command post exercise was carried out, and combined training included a small-scale exercise and antisubmarine training on several occasions. These activities were carried out on the high seas near Japan, including the Sea of Japan. Maritime Self-Defense Force ships also began to supply bunker oil to the U.S. Navy ships in late 1983 and continued to do so. In May and June 1984, a large naval exercise was staged in the central Pacific and in the area between Hawaii and San Diego. Around eighty ships, 250 aircraft, and more than 50,000 personnel from the United States, Australia, Canada, New Zealand, and Japan participated. This RIMPAC (Rim of the Pacific) Exercise would be repeated in subsequent years.

Throughout the 1980s, the Ground Self-Defense Force continued to conduct command post exercises and field training exercises with U.S. forces. In September 1986, some eighty Japanese Ground Self-Defense Force personnel and another 250 from the U.S. military participated in command post exercises in Hawaii. In January 1987, another joint command post exercise was conducted in Sendai.[13] Along with more RIMPAC exercises in 1986, the Air Self-Defense Force began command post exercises in 1983 and 1984 to cooperate with its U.S. counterpart. In 1986, the Air Self-Defense Force conducted air-defense combat training three times, with fighter combat training on ten occasions.

The nature of the U.S.-Japanese alliance, in which one initiates and the other follows, creates political-psychological problems for the Japanese officer corps. On the one hand, the Japanese officers regard the Pentagon as an ally in lobbying the Japanese government for improved funding and acquisitions. But on the other hand, the Pentagon bureaucracy has an interest in keeping the Self-Defense Forces under control. At a time when trade friction between the two countries is giving rise to acrimonious debate, the tension spills over into defense cooperation. Since defense and trade are the two major ties in the bilateral relations, the Japanese officer corps feel the peculiar strain.

The 1977 defense debate started by Prime Minister Fukuda had its origin among the Japanese officer corps, which sought to improve its collective status through coordination with its counterpart in the U.S. Department of Defense.[14] This is nothing new. In postwar Japan, Washington has always been the prime mover behind military expansion as well as restraint. For instance, there have been periodic warnings against Japan's going nuclear, though the nuclear question never became an issue because of Japan's self-abnegation. In the past, the Pentagon and the National Security Council have always sought to dampen trade disputes and to prevent them from spilling over into defense cooperation. Lately, however, the Pentagon has become acutely concerned over the American loss of competitive edge in defense-related industries. In the spring of 1987, the Pentagon reversed itself and began to intervene in trade disputes as an active participant. It vetoed the acquisition of Fairchild, a French chip maker, by Japan's Fujitsu. The Pentagon also vetoed Japan's plan to manufacture the next generation of fighter aircraft, designated FSX, which enjoyed wide support in Japan's industries and Self-Defense Forces officer corps.

Ultimately, the tension in the officer corps can be traced to the fact that Japan's excessive dependence on U.S. protection deprives it of autonomy and places it at the mercy of Washington's policy. The Japanese fighting men may take their jobs seriously, but their countrymen tend to regard them not as forces of national defense in their own right but a means to keep the protector in good humor. As long as the United States remains the mainstay of Japan's security, a dependency syndrome will gnaw at the morale of the Self-Defense Forces. The best and the brightest in postwar Japan, therefore, seek occupations that enable them to pursue excellence in freedom. These are in higher civil service in nondefense ministries, commerce, and industry. According to internal critics, a careerist attitude is said to be pervasive among the uniformed officers. The problem begins with the self-selection process for the applicants to the Defense College, which combines West Point, Annapolis, and the Air Academy of the United States into one.

Current Japanese Defense Strategy

As we have noted in Chapter 2, the Japanese government's foreign and defense policies changed substantially in the wake of the crises in Iran and Afghanistan. Public and Diet debate on national defense was further intensified. There was a great deal of confusion and disagreement on the nature of the Soviet threat, assessment of the American countervailing power, and appropriate strategy for Japan. Recently, however, different opinions coalesced into a consensus—as far as the establishment was concerned—with the appearance of a tract written by Hisahiko Okazaki, a senior Foreign Ministry official who has served as a councilor at the Defense Agency in the recent past. Because his ideas still represent the dominant thinking in the government and the establishment today, they will serve as a benchmark against which to assess other approaches that have appeared since.[15]

Okazaki agrees with the majority of strategic thinkers in the West on the changing nature of nuclear deterrence. The phenomenal increase in Soviet strategic arsenals in the 1960s and early 1970s has created basic parity in the deterrence capability of the two superpowers. If the United States had ever had the ability to fight and win a thermonuclear exchange in the days of superiority, it was now gone. Strategic nuclear arsenals still serve their purpose in deterring the other side from using them, but the threshold is high. America's "threat to commit suicide," Kissinger told the Japanese in 1983, "does not deter" conventional attacks. Local defense must rely on conventional arms.

It follows that Japan still needs the U.S. nuclear umbrella to prevent Soviet nuclear blackmail. But Japan can no longer rely on that umbrella alone to enjoy security as in the past. For the first time, conventional arms are in demand in their own right rather than as a tripwire or mere shield. With or without "nuclear allergy," most Japanese accept this thesis. There is one exceptional circumstance, however, and it will be dealt with below.

In light of the nuclear parity, Okazaki goes on to explain precisely the nature of the threat posed by the Soviet buildup in Asia since the late 1960s. There was, he says, a rapid buildup in the late 1960s and early 1970s, followed by a leveling off in the mid-1970s, and finally another significant increase in the areas east of Lake Baikal from the late 1970s through the early 1980s.[16] The first expansion, consisting of 21 divisions along the border with China, can be attributed to the Sino-Soviet tension. But the latest expansion was unmistakably directed at the combination of U.S., Chinese, and Japanese powers, and it was part of a worldwide renewal and expansion of Soviet forces. In fact, deployment of aircraft and ships to the Pacific fleet exceeded that to other regions because this fleet was in charge of the Sea of Okhotsk, Cam Ranh Bay, the Indian Ocean, the South China Sea, and the Persian Gulf. Two aircraft carriers of the Minsk class, amphibious landing ships, and the fortification of Japan's Northern Territories were convincing proof of the Soviet Union's new interest.

Having sufficiently alarmed the audience, Okazaki then reassures them by saying that joining the global network of Western alliances would be adequate to meet Japan's security needs, a point of view that the Gaimushō, Okazaki's home ministry, accepted after the Soviet invasion of Afghanistan. He maintains that all that Japan need do is not be the weakest link in the chain. This is so because Japan is not likely to be the primary object of a Soviet attack. The NATO front in Europe or even the Persian Gulf, he thinks, has higher priority for Moscow. Moreover, China's presence along an extended border creates a diversionary effect. For Okazaki's purpose, it matters little whether Peking restores diplomatic cordiality with Moscow. As long as a Sino-Soviet military alliance does not exist—and one will not come, according to him—the Soviet Union will have to reserve nearly one-half of its strength in the Far East to deter the Chinese while engaging elsewhere.[17]

Then what are the circumstances that warrant a Soviet attack on Japan? Neither Okazaki nor anyone else, it seems, can write a credible scenario for an isolated Soviet invasion of Japan as long as the U.S.-Japanese security treaty exists. But let us assume the impossible. While holding the NATO and the Chinese fronts, can the Soviets marshal ten divisions? That is a rather high figure. If they hold one half of that in reserve, five divisions will be used for assault. The assumption behind the National Defense Program Outline of a "limited and small-scale" Soviet aggression consisting of two to five divisions originates in such a reckoning. Mobilization of men, materiel, and ships on the other shore is bound to be detected in advance, so the chances for a surprise are slight. Even if the Japanese insist on the principle of "passive defense" in the face of imminent danger—which is unlikely—the invaders must survive American naval and air counterattacks. The conclusion is that an isolated invasion is highly unlikely. The ocean—even if only forty kilometers wide at some points—is a great barrier.

The only conceivable scenario is in the context of a full-scale U.S.-Soviet war or a third world war, triggered by events in other regions. If the Reagan administration acts on its war plans of horizontal escalation, the war will instantly spread worldwide. If the United States confines it to the originating theater, Okazaki points out, the Soviets will nonetheless involve Japan at the outset. He sees two reasons for this. One is Japan's inherent value because of its geopolitical, strategic position—it sits astride the choke points that Soviet ships must transit in order to carry out their strategic missions against the United States.

Through the 1970s, the range of submarine-launched ballistic missiles was such that a Soviet submarine had to exit from the Sea of Japan to the high seas before firing them. Since then, the reach of Soviet SLBMs has been extended, and they can be fired from areas closer to home. The Sea of Okhotsk, nestled under the Kamchatka Peninsula, and the submarine base in Petropavlovsk acquired enormous significance. But even then the Petropavlovsk base must be supplied by sea through the choke points. Japan's ability to close them off makes it an important strategic object in the Soviet view, says Okazaki.

The second reason given by Okazaki to sustain his Japan-in-World-War-III scenario is not so hard and fast. Whether Japan will be attacked or not, he says, depends on the cost. He knows that if Japan had an offensive capability, it could persuade the Soviets to desist from opening a second front.[18] Even if not, a thoroughgoing conventional defense might deter the Soviets from overrunning the choke points or occupying Hokkaido. This is where Okazaki is constrained by his status as a Foreign Ministry official—he cannot argue for nuclear deterrence. But the point is critical. According to his scenario, a Japanese prime minister must order the blockade of three straits—all of which hug the public, international waters in the midst—to the Sea of Japan under circumstances where the Soviets offered no direct provocation to Japan. Washington will put pressure on him with the assurance that it will deter Soviet retaliation, nuclear or otherwise. Prime Minister Nakasone intimated that he would close the straits, but could he carry the nation with him?

If war comes, Okazaki thinks, it will remain subnuclear and not be pushed to a decisive conclusion. That is, after fighting that may conceptually resemble the Korean War, with the front moving back and forth, the two superpowers will seek a modus vivendi and ceasefire when and where it is optimal. Japan's interest, Okazaki points out correctly, is to see to it that no part of its territory falls to the Soviet side at the point where the United States loses interest in fighting.

Okazaki is a hawk in the Foreign Ministry, but his book was widely acclaimed and had few enemies. Wisely enough, he left to experts the question of tonnage of ships, number of aircraft, or divisions required for his strategy. He did not touch on tactical matters either. In fact, he has little to say on blockading straits or on sea-lane defense. Perhaps one reason why he was so well received was because indirectly he assured the basic adequacy of the existing defense establishment. He expressly rested himself on the premise that no constitutional change was necessary to do what he recommended. This means that sea-lane defense—calling for operation on the high seas—has a marginal status in his strategy. When all is said and done, his call, "all the way with the United States in the third world war," has on the contrary a reassuring ring. Nothing short of another world war, it seems, need worry Japan.

But that is not quite so. Okazaki adds a subjective element: the need to keep the Americans, or the Anglo-Saxons as he calls them, well disposed toward keeping their worldwide commitments. What Japan needs to do under this rubric he does not say. It may be that he felt sea-lane defense was unnecessary and irrelevant if the straits were blockaded, but that it must nonetheless be maintained for the sake of allied comity.

The so-called sea-lane defense emerged as a major subject of debate in Japan when Prime Minister Suzuki committed himself to it during his visit with President Reagan in May 1981, shortly before Okazaki's book appeared in print. The debate concerns just what sea-lane defense is and what it was that Japan committed itself to.[19] At a bilateral conference of defense bureaucracies in June, CINCPAC expanded on Suzuki's commitment to include air cover over "sea lanes." Then CINCPAC vigorously pushed for integration of the Maritime Self-Defense Force with the Seventh Fleet and created a falling-out between the Maritime Self-Defense Force and the other two services, which are more interested in local defense of Japan.

It took agonizing debates in the Diet to commit Japan to sea-lane defense because that calls for operations on the high seas. Moreover, the Japanese understanding of sea-lane defense was at odds with the CINCPAC's. Ever since sea-lane defense was postulated during the Third Defense Buildup, it meant defense of civilian commerce and supplies against interdiction and raid. But naturally defense against commerce raiders is not what interested the Seventh Fleet, though the point was underplayed, perhaps because it was politically sensitive in Japan. The United States Navy under its sprightly Secretary, John E. Lehman, Jr., author of the so-called "Maritime Strategy," was interested primarily in keeping open the sea lines of communication to Japan and to the Indian Ocean for offensive purposes. The U.S. Navy's carrier-based battle group was not bound to any specific lane, and it demanded Japanese help in anti-submarine warfare to make possible a forward deployment around Japan. Amid a heated debate in Tokyo as to what was agreed to, the annual RIMPAC joint exercises were launched, and the Maritime Self-Defense Force became in a few years an integrated arm of the Seventh Fleet. The Air Self-Defense Force stood somewhere between the antisubmarine-warfare-bound navy and the homebound army. The air force postulated for itself a role in providing air cover over the sea lanes, presumably against Soviet Backfire bombers, and it is building an air base on Iwo Jima. But it has not been able to integrate itself with the Seventh Fleet with zeal.

Several reasons account for this development. The major initial impetus to U.S. and Japanese military expansion was provided by the Soviet invasion of Afghanistan, which threatened Iran and the Persian Gulf. Protection of the Persian Gulf and the sea lanes between it and Europe and Japan became the immediate concern of the United States. Hasty organization of the Rapid Deployment Force was one answer. In this context Japan's Maritime Self-Defense Force came in for special attention. In addition, CINCPAC is a command in which the U.S. Navy's presence overshadows that of the U.S. Army. It is perhaps for this reason that U.S.-Japanese integration and cooperation developed first among the seaborne services. Because the Pentagon and CINCPAC have been the most effective lobby for Japan's arms buildup, the Maritime Self-Defense Force's interest in acquiring more ships and a larger budget was well served by cooperating with them.[20]

Given the U.S. dominance in the alliance, a degree of integration of Japanese forces with their American counterparts is almost inevitable. Conceptually, integration is justified by the division of labor whereby Japan will provide the shield and the United States the sword. But functional integration should not override the desirability of allied cooperation. The point of allied cooperation has been and ought to be to elicit greater self-help from Japan in conventional defense. There is no substitute for Japanese self-help. If integration would divide Japan's already scarce military resources and demoralize the Japanese military, it must be moderated.

The problem of sea-lane defense is that it is only indirectly related to local defense of Japan. Japan's survival in war depends on local defense. Foreign naval and air arms may not ensure Japan's territorial integrity. In China, Korea, and Vietnam the final conclusions were arrived at through ground fighting, but U.S. air and naval superiority was never in doubt. In the immediate aftermath of the Afghanistan invasion, the so-called swing strategy—whereby U.S. naval resources would swing between the Atlantic and Pacific theaters, depending on Soviet threat—was still openly acknowledged to be in effect. Without the Seventh Fleet in the northwestern Pacific, Japan's navy—trained to escort the American ships—serves little purpose. More important, without forward deployment of U.S. offensive capability, Japan would have no assurance of deterrence against Soviet reaction to the blockading of straits.

This was the state of affairs until about 1984. The initial alarm over Afghanistan subsided, and the "window of vulnerability" was pronounced closed, following a painful debate over various deployment modes for the MX missile. Strategic analysts in the West have had a chance to take another look at the Soviet Union. In Japan, a bright young officer of the Ground Self-Defense Force Staff Office, Lt. Col. Shigeki Nishimura, came up with a revised assessment of Soviet strategy along with a recommended counter-strategy for Japan. Nishimura's basic framework was Okazaki's diagnosis and prescription. But in revising and refining it, Nishimura arrived at a strategy that can enlist the three services as an integrated whole for a "forward" deployment.[21]

Nishimura posits the so-called Nordic analogy to explain the geopolitical predicament of northern Japan as it has confronted Soviet expansion since the 1970s. He points out that both Norway and northern Japan share this fact in common: they are contiguous to the area where Soviet missile submarines are deployed, and they control the choke points against the Soviet navy. In both regions the Soviets have been advancing outward from the hinterland in concentric circles of defense zones. In the Japanese case, the inner zone—enjoying tactical air cover—includes the Sea of Japan and the Sea of Okhotsk. The Okhotsk is the area of submarine deployment, but it can only be supplied from Vladivostok by ships passing through the Soya or Tsugaru straits, of which only Tsugaru remains ice-free year round. In wartime, the Soviets must try to control at least one channel for free passage. That means occupying northern Hokkaido or all of Hokkaido plus northern Honshu. The Hokkaido island, Nishimura feels, protrudes uncomfortably into a vital defense zone of the Soviet Union, bisecting two bodies of water that are really one.

The outer zone of defense encompasses all of Japan and extends far out into the Pacific; its perimeter is co-extensive with the operating radius of Backfire bombers and attack submarines. Their mission is to disrupt allied sea lines of communication, deny access to U.S. carrier battle groups, and isolate Japan.

The Soviet Pacific fleet is assigned two vital tasks to perform in the area under its control. One is to husband and protect its fleet of missile-launching submarines as a strategic reserve in a war with the United States. Nishimura shares Okazaki's hope that thermonuclear exchange will be avoided in such a contingency, but if the Soviet Union presses its advantage in conventional strength on NATO's front, the United States may be tempted to eliminate Soviet submarine-launched ballistic missiles to cancel out the Soviet upper hand. Because of the nature of Soviet submarines as a strategic reserve vital to Soviet survival, Japan now has the distinction of being as important to the Soviet calculus as Western Europe, even though, Nishimura concedes, the war in Europe will be the third world war.

The other task of the Soviet Fleet is not so much power projection as interdiction of U.S. power projection into Southwest Asia. The United States can fight in the Gulf by securing the dangerously extended sea lines of communication to the region. The task of cutting off sea lines of communication would fall squarely on the Soviet fleet based in Vladivostok. A war that involves the Seventh Fleet against the Soviet Pacific fleet can hardly leave Japan untouched, Nishimura argues. If a war in the Persian Gulf cannot be localized, it may spread more easily to East Asia than to Europe because there is less risk of nuclear escalation in the former. While a war triggered by events in the Third World is likely to remain subnuclear, in Nishimura's reckoning, the Soviets may try to compensate for their naval weaknesses by instigating a diversionary war in Korea. Another war in Korea would force the Chinese to support Pyongyang, dissolve Sino-Soviet tension, and liquidate Sino-American detente.

A war in Korea in the context of a world war would tax Japan to the hilt, because it would amount to a two-front war. Nishimura's northern strategy rests on the assumption that the Republic of Korea's forces, the U.S. Second Division, and the U.S. Marine Corps reserve on Okinawa would hold the line in Korea. A two-front war would be a grave contingency for Japan. If anything, the nuclear parity between the two superpowers has increased the chances for multifront, conventional, limited wars.

Limited or unlimited, Nishimura maintains, a U.S.-Soviet conflict anywhere will automatically lead to Soviet occupation of northern Japan. The Soviet threat is inherent in Japan's geographical position and in nothing else. In so arguing, Nishimura goes further than Okazaki, who felt that there are circumstances in which Japan could bargain for neutrality in wars elsewhere. In this author's judgment, Okazaki's point remains valid against Nishimura. Unless the Soviet Union intends to take all of Japan, it would be foolhardy to provoke it simply by virtue of its geographical position. A political negotiation by means of carrot and stick to induce Japan's neutrality seems well worth the effort, since it would not only mean safe transit but also the end of the U.S.-Japanese alliance and possibly Japan's Finlandization as well.

Nonetheless, if any U.S.-Soviet conflict anywhere automatically entails Soviet invasion of Hokkaido and possibly also northern Honshu, three things follow. First, the Ground Self-Defense Force—by far the most nationalistic of all the services—has found a mission in which it can play a dominant and central role, and with which the other two services must integrate themselves. Second, the northern strategy does not displace sea-lane defense. On the contrary, it provides a credible rationale for sea-lane defense by relating the survival of the forward-deployed Seventh Fleet specifically to Japan's own survival. Third, the interests of Japan, the United States, and Western Europe become virtually identical, or at least inseparable: de facto, Japan has become a member of NATO.

Whether this point is really accepted or whether it is a means of advancing the Ground Self-Defense Force's interest is difficult to say.[22] The fact remains, however, that for the first time not only the Ground Self-Defense Force but all three services have found an integrated plan that is meaningfully and credibly related to Japan's defense. This is just the beginning, but two new trends are visible. One is an ever-expanding bundle of joint planning, exercises, and cooperation between the American and Japanese armed forces. A joint war plan and rules of engagement have been formally approved.[23] Because the Self-Defense Forces as a whole have found a convincing mission, they will gradually shift their tactics away from the absurd political straitjacket of shoreline defense.

Next we will deal with the issues of the nuclear umbrella. Japan's policies toward nuclear weapons are still basically a compromise between the allergy against them and the desire to have their protection: Japan pretends that nuclear weapons have not been "introduced" onto its soil, so long as the United States remains silent. There is little public debate over nuclear weapons except as a peace issue. Within the Self-Defense Forces, there is a subsurface tension caused by the absence of *the* weapon. The tension is structural: anyone who takes defense seriously would want to control the full range of weapons. The tension has been managed with the assumption that the United States will provide nuclear deterrence. The trouble is that the United States cannot admit to moving nuclear weapons into Japan. This should be a cause for outcry against decoupling, but the Japanese remain silent. The United States cannot negotiate with the Soviets for mutual reduction of weapons it cannot claim to possess. But Japan's quiescence is not necessarily peculiar to it—both China and South Korea have been quieter about Soviet nuclear weapons than they could have been.[24]

There is a great asymmetry between Soviet nuclear deployment and the American umbrella over Japan. Soviet SS-20s and Backfire bombers are widely dispersed over a sparsely populated territory with no large urban concentration that can be held hostage. Japan is the polar opposite. Since Japan has formally declined theater nuclear defense, it is arguably decoupled from protection by U.S. strategic arsenals. Yet the quirk of the Japanese nuclear allergy is such that Japan is vigilant against American weapons but silent against Soviet buildup. Fortunately, in September 1987 the United States and the Soviet Union agreed to conclude a treaty banning intermediate-range nuclear forces, but its implications for Japan and Asia are yet to be fully analyzed.

Until now, the Japanese government's attitude has been governed mostly by the desire to accommodate the nuclear allergy. To quote from Professor Kosaka, the author of the comprehensive-security concept and adviser to several prime ministers in the past:

> It would be unnecessary in military terms, and counterproductive politically, to overreact to these deployments [of SS-20s and Backfires] by rushing to field "equivalent" weapons systems—and thereby stir up public anxieties about a presumed heightened nuclear threat. One of the dilemmas of dealing with the nuclear issue is that a response of deploying equivalent military systems would doubly play into Soviets hands: it would advertise Moscow's enhanced nuclear deployments, . . . it would also stimulate antinuclear political pressures in allied countries.[25]

But whether this policy will be workable in the future remains to be seen. Until the latest U.S.-Soviet accord on INF superseded the agreement at Reykjavik, the Soviets were permitted to transfer 100 SS-20s to east of the Urals. But there was no reaction from Japan's peace movement. The decline of nuclear hysteria seems to have turned the Japanese into quiet bystanders, at least for now.

But in contrast, Japan is ever alert to relations with the United States. The worsening trade disputes with the United States over the last few years, culminating in the first trade sanction against Japan in 1987, have produced what could be the beginning of Japan's reorientation away from export-dependence to a domestic-demand-pull economy, a remarkable feat. The Japanese have been uncomfortable with the popular Congressional habit of attributing Japan's trade surplus to its alleged military free ride. Because Japan's defense is tied to America's, if the Americans feel they are in decline, the Japanese have to compensate for it—even if the Soviets are on the retreat. So it is that Okazaki, the former ambassador to Saudi Arabia, proposed in early 1988 a significant upward revision of Japan's defense within the Foreign Ministry and a committee of the Liberal Democratic Party. The crux of the proposal consists of the concept of "required defense capability" (*shoyō bōeiryoku*), which displaces the concept of a standard defense force and its political corollary, the concept of comprehensive security.

The standard defense force is geared not to Soviet capabilities but to Soviet intentions, and it will be expanded if Soviet intentions toward Japan turn hostile. In the meantime, comprehensive security augments the shortfall of military defense with nonmilitary policies such as diplomacy and foreign aid. At least this was the theory behind Japan's current buildup. Okazaki seeks to scuttle this approach and gear Japan's defense to Soviet capabilities. It is too early to tell what will follow in strategy and military planning, but he is talking of a defense expenditure in the neighborhood of 1.5 percent of GNP. Such an increase may be devoted to expanded sea-lane defense, which we propose in the next chapter.[26]

Notes

1. The movement was initiated by former prime minister Konoye. See his letter cited in Ryūichi Nagao (ed.), *Nihon Kempō shi* [History of Japan's Constitutions] (Tokyo: Tokyo University Press, 1976), pp. 330–331.

2. Ikuhiko Hata, *Shiroku saigunbi* [History of Rearmament] (Tokyo: Bungei Shunjūsha, 1976), pp. 151–155.

3. Yōzo Katō, *Shiroku Jieitai-shi* [A Biographical History of the Self-Defense Forces] (Tokyo: Gekkan Seisaku, 1979), pp. 36–37.

4. Ibid., p. 118.

5. Ibid., pp. 120–121.

6. Ibid., pp. 114–117.

7. Kiyofuku Chūma, *Saigunbi no seiji-gaku* [The Politics of Rearmament] (Tokyo: Chishiki-sha, 1985), p. 97.

8. The issue that touched off his protest was the long-standing injunction against ASDF interceptors firing on intruding foreign military aircraft. If a pilot does fire, he does so at his own risk under the rubric of "citizen's arrest."

9. Hideo Ōtake, *Nihon no bōei to kokunai seiji* [Japan's Defense and Domestic Politics] (Tokyo: Sanichi Shobō, 1983), p. 191.

10. This reform is uniformly endorsed by those whom we have interviewed in the officer corps.

11. Defense Agency, *Defense of Japan, 1988* (Tokyo: The Japan Times, 1988).

12. For an excellent account of this process, see Hideo Ōtake, *Nihon no bōei to kokunai seiji.*

13. Hisahiko Okazaki, *Senryaku-teki shikō towa nanika* [What Is Strategic Thinking?] (Tokyo: Chūō Kōronsha, 1983).

14. Ibid., p. 151.

15. Ibid., pp. 157–160.

16. Hisahiko Okazaki, "Nihon bōei no tame no kihon senryaku" [The Basic Strategy for Defending Japan], *Voice,* September 1983, pp. 64–81.

17. See the prime minister's remarks at the press conference in Washington, cited in Hideo Ōtake, p. 363.

18. *Asahi Shimbun,* June 24, 1981, p. 1.

19. Kiyofuku Chūma, *Saigunbi no seiji-gaku,* pp. 108–124.

20. In one major instance of cooperation, which may be the pattern for all the others, the Japanese services gave their shopping list to the Pentagon, which in

turn lobbied for that list with the Japanese government. Kiyofuku Chūma, *Saigunbi no seiji-gaku,* pp. 89–91.

21. Shigeki Nishimura, "Nihon no bōei senryaku o kangaeru: gurōbaru-apurōchi ni yoru hoppo zenpō bōei-ron" [Thinking About Japan's Defense Strategy: The Forward Defense of the North Through a Global Approach], *Shin Bōei Ronshū,* July 1984, pp. 50–79.

22. Even in the U.S. Navy, Lehman's Maritime Strategy seems to have many silent critics. They are keeping their heads down for the time being because they all stand to benefit from the 600-ship navy he has been pushing for. His critics charge that he is provoking the Soviets. See "Lehman's Sea-War Strategy Is Alive, But for How Long?" *New York Times,* March 23, 1987, p. 8.

23. *Asahi Shimbun,* December 24, 1984, p. 3.

24. Richard H. Solomon and Masataka Kosaka, "Nuclear Dilemmas and Asian Security: Problems of Coalition Defense in The Nuclear Era," in Richard H. Solomon and Masataka Kosaka (eds.), *The Soviet Far East Military Buildup: Nuclear Dilemmas and Asian Security* (Dover, Mass.: Auburn House Publishing Company, 1986), p. 8.

25. Ibid., p. 13.

26. Hisahiko Okazaki, "Magarikado ni kita Nichi-Bei dōmei" [The Japan-U.S. Alliance at a Crossroads], *Bungei Shunjū,* July 1988, pp. 94–111.

7

America's Defense of Asia and the Pacific Basin

A rarely mentioned but direct benefit of the U.S.-Japanese security relationship for Japan is the long-term protection of the sea routes that extend between Japan and North and South America and between Japan and the Suez Canal and the Middle East.

In fact, all of the Asian and Pacific countries and territories have benefited from the vast security system created and maintained by the United States from World War II until the present. This area's foreign trade, which depends upon the many sea routes for commerce, serves as an engine for the economic growth and national survival of nearly all Asian and Pacific countries and territories. In fact, no modernizing country or territory can survive for long without foreign trade. The region's foreign trade is mainly transported by a huge merchant marine that must have safe access to the sea routes linking the Indian and Pacific oceans to the rest of the world. These sea routes pass through nearly a half-dozen straits and canals that connect the Indian and Pacific oceans to the final sources of supply and markets for the area.

This security system has two major components, which are closely connected. One functions to maintain the defense of Japan; supports South Korea's defenses; provides for the security of the Philippines and its Association of Southeast Asian Nations (ASEAN) neighbors, the Pacific Ocean territories, Australia, and New Zealand; and guarantees safe access to Middle East oil and shipping use of the sea lines connecting with the Suez and Panama canals. The other functions to defend the security of North American territories in the eastern Pacific.

Both components of this vast security system have produced tangible benefits for the Asian and Pacific countries and territories, especially the safe passage of merchant marine via the Asian-Pacific sea lines of communication.

TABLE 7.1

Gross Domestic Product and Foreign Trade of Asian Countries
as a Percentage of World GDP and Foreign Trade (1983)

Country or Country Group	(1) GDP (U.S.$ million)	(2) Percent of World GDP	(3) Foreign Trade Value (U.S.$ million)	(4) Foreign Trade as % of GNP	(5) Percent of World Trade
Socialist countries[a]	422,600	11.4	49,010	11.6	1.3
Japan	1,157,456	8.5	273,060	23.61	7.4
Australia	168,366	1.2	40,080	23.8	1.1
New Zealand	23,368	0.2	11,617	49.7	0.3
Developing countries and territories of Asia[b]	1,073,154	7.9	616,715	57.5	16.7
Developing countries and territories of Oceania[c]	5,702	0.05	4,540	79.6	0.1
TOTAL	2,850,646	21.0	984,847	34.5	26.6

a. Includes only People's Republic of China and Democratic People's Republic of Korea; excludes Vietnam and Mongolia.

b. Excludes Macao.

c. Excludes American Samoa, Guam, Samoa, and Vanuatu.

Sources: 1. United Nations, *Statistical Yearbook, 1983/1984,* (New York: United Nations, 1986), p. 95 for GDP.
2. United Nations, *Handbook of International Trade and Development Statistics, 1986. Supplement,* (New York: United Nations, 1987), Tables 1.1 and 1.2.
3. Republic of China, *Taiwan Statistical Data Book, 1985,* (Taipei: Council for Economic Planning and Development, 1985), p. 21 and pp. 328–329.

The Importance of the
Asian-Pacific Sea Lines of Communication

Consider the Asia-Pacific of 1983. The gross domestic product, or total value of all goods and services, produced by all countries and territories of the Asian-Pacific region came to roughly $2.8 trillion (Table 7.1, col. 1). This sum amounted to about 21 percent of the world's gross domestic product. Much of the region's total output, however, depended upon foreign trade. If we take exports and imports as total foreign trade, Asia's foreign trade amounted to around one-third of its gross domestic product. Foreign trade proved to be much more important for Asia's developing countries (Table 7.1, col. 4). Traditionally, socialist states based on central planning have depended upon foreign trade for only a small component of gross domestic product. Yet even China's foreign trade began to grow rapidly after 1978, and now trade strongly influences the economic development of certain provinces in that huge economy. Finally, Asia's total foreign trade as a share of world trade reached nearly 27 percent, and it will probably climb in the next decade if the growth rates for the Pacific Basin countries remains as high as in the recent past (Table 7.1, col. 5).

The trade in certain critical commodities determines the economic well-being and security of Asia and the Pacific countries and territories. For example, roughly 50 percent of Asia's oil comes by sea from the Persian Gulf through the three straits in Southeast Asia. Chart 1 shows that in the mid-1980s the Middle East supplied 2.8 million barrels of oil per day to Asia, another 0.6 million barrels to North America, and 0.7 million barrels to South America through the sea lanes of the Indian and Pacific oceans. Similarly, Indonesia supplied 0.9 and 0.4 million barrels of oil per day to Japan and the United States, respectively, through the various Pacific Ocean sea routes. The Middle East also supplies liquefied natural gas in great quantities to India and Japan. Again, coal from North America, Australia, and South Africa moves along the various sea routes to supply Japan's needs.

Of the Asian and the Pacific countries, Japan benefits most from the uninterrupted flow of shipping from distant sources of supplies and markets. Again, in 1983 Japan produced some 40 percent of Asia's GDP and 8.5 percent of the world's GDP; those figures are even higher today. Foreign trade also gave a powerful boost to Japan's economy, and without access to supplies of raw materials and markets for its manufactured goods and services, Japan could not have achieved the economic superpower status it now has. Chart 2 shows the importance of the sea routes by which Japan's foreign trade is conducted. These routes allow Japanese ships and those of other states to transport goods between Japan and North and South America, and through the Panama Canal to Europe and elsewhere. There are also routes that link Japan to Southeast Asia and Australia. And finally, there are routes that enable Japan to acquire

Chart 1   Pacific Basin oil trade (million barrels per day, 1985)

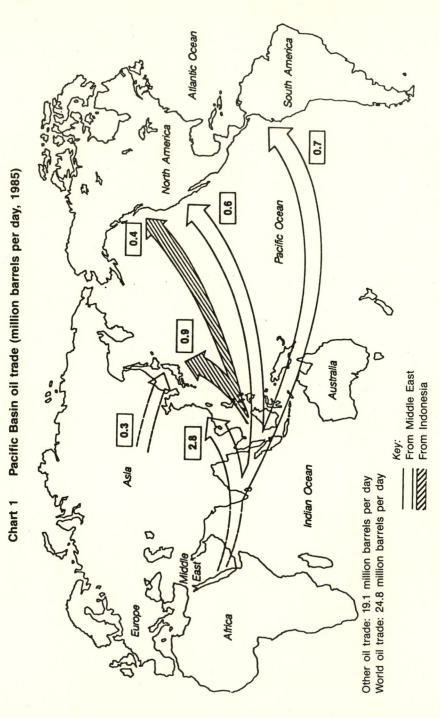

Other oil trade: 19.1 million barrels per day
World oil trade: 24.8 million barrels per day

Key:
From Middle East
From Indonesia

Source: British Petroleum Statistical Review of the World Oil Industry, June 1985, p. 16.

Chart 2: Japan: The Security of Its Sea Routes

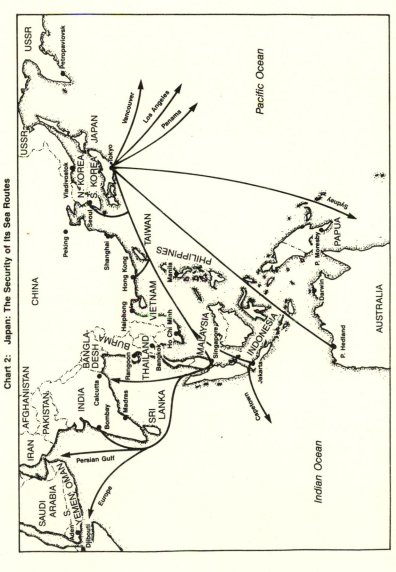

Chart 3: Japan's Industrial Areas and Key Imports (early 1980s)

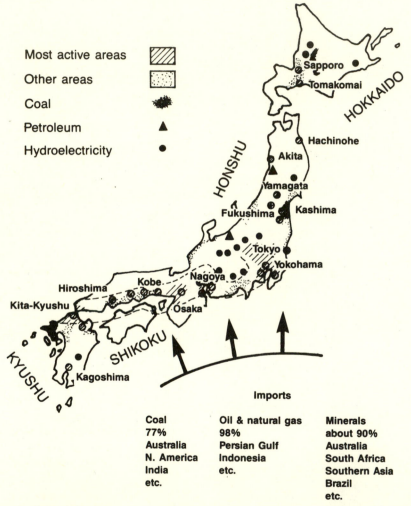

Most active areas

Other areas

Coal

Petroleum

Hydroelectricity

HOKKAIDO

Sapporo

Tomakomai

Hachinohe

Akita

Yamagata

Kashima

HONSHU

Fukushima

Tokyo

Yokohama

Hiroshima

Kobe

Nagoya

Kita-Kyushu

Osaka

SHIKOKU

KYUSHU

Kagoshima

Imports

Coal	Oil & natural gas	Minerals
77%	98%	about 90%
Australia	Persian Gulf	Australia
N. America	Indonesia	South Africa
India	etc.	Southern Asia
etc.		Brazil
		etc.

Source: Gérard Chaliard and Jean-Pierre Rageau, *A Strategic Atlas: Comparative Geo-politics of the World's Powers,* second edition, revised and updated (New York: Harper & Row, 1985), p. 155. Copyright © 1983 by Librairie Arthème Fayard. English translation copyright © 1985 by Gérard Chaliard and Jean-Pierre Rageau. Reprinted by permission of Harper & Row, Publishers, Inc.

much-needed oil from the Middle East and to trade with Europe through the Suez Canal.

But it is Chart 3 that shows the strategic importance of these sea routes. Japan's many industrial areas are located on four small islands. Those industrial areas depend on the flow of raw materials for the energy and inputs so necessary for modern enterprises to produce goods and services for domestic consumption and foreign export. Japan must import about 77 percent of its coal from Australia, North America, India, and elsewhere; 98 percent of the oil and natural gas the country consumes must come from the Persian Gulf, Indonesia, and elsewhere; and about 90 percent of the minerals needed for industry come from Australia, South Africa, South Asia, and South America. In 1983, oceangoing ships transported 85 percent of Japan's $147 billion worth of exports and 90 percent of its $112.7 billion worth of imports.[1] Although Japan began as early as 1972 to develop substitutes for oil-derived energy in order to reduce its dependence upon overseas oil, even by the year 2000 it will still have to import 42 percent of all its energy needs, mostly in oil.[2] Therefore, of all the Asian and Pacific countries and territories, Japan depends most upon foreign trade and the safe passage of ships along the Asian-Pacific sea lines of communication.

The U.S. Security System in Asia

These sea lines of communication, upon which Japan and other Asian and Pacific countries and territories so greatly depend for their economic prosperity and security, have been protected by a huge, far-flung network of U.S. military bases and treaties with various countries that allow the United States to use those bases. The U.S. naval forces, air wings, ground forces, support services, and information-gathering capabilities depend upon this system of bases and their maintenance. In effect, this security system of military bases produces a public good that we can define as security. That public good has served the interests of the United States just as it has benefited the Asian and Pacific countries and territories, even though some countries and territories have naturally benefited more than others. What does this system look like?

The military bases on the western coast of the United States support the eastern Pacific component of this system. These bases include naval air stations and airfields at Adak Island in Alaska, seven stations and airfields in California, and one in Hawaii.[3] In addition, there are naval airfields and bases in the same area: one at Adak, four in California, one in Hawaii. There are also three naval shipyards: one each in Hawaii, California, and Washington state. Finally, there are a number of Marine Corps air stations, helicopter facilities, and bases in Hawaii and California. Moving westward from the United States, we first come to the bases in Guam and the Philippines. Then we move northward to the U.S. naval stations, shipyards, Air Force bases, and other facilities in Okinawa,

South Korea, and Japan. Turning to the distant south, we find the U.S. satellite tracking stations in Australia. Then we move across the Indian Ocean to the U.S. base on Diego Garcia, leased from Britain; and finally, to the ports located in Kuwait and Egypt, where the U.S. Navy can now call and where U.S. personnel are stationed.

To defend this network of bases, the United States maintains two fleets, the Third and the Seventh, in the Pacific. The Sixth Fleet, located in the Mediterranean, was partly deployed to the Persian Gulf in 1987–1988 to provide escort for ships flying the U.S. flag. Some vessels of the U.S. Seventh Fleet now serve in the Indian Ocean: one carrier and five other vessels were there in 1987.[4] Nuclear submarines with ballistic missile-launch capabilities are also based in the Pacific.

Meanwhile, U.S. ground forces are located in Hawaii, Japan, South Korea, and Okinawa. Various air wings are based in Japan, the Philippines, South Korea, Hawaii, and Guam. United States P-3Cs fly surveillance missions over the Pacific and Indian oceans every week to monitor ship movements. U.S. earth satellites gather additional information on defense forces belonging to other states.

By the mid-1980s, the United States was conducting naval and air exercises with various allies in the waters of Southeast Asia, the western and mid-Pacific, and around Japan. These exercises were designed to develop rapid military deployment capability for U.S. military forces to different oceans if any aggressor tried to disrupt sea route traffic. Another purpose was to develop procedures for protecting oceangoing traffic through the straits of Southeast Asia as well as to prevent the exodus of Soviet ships through the straits around Japan in the event of a major war.

Providing sea route protection is only one of the many functions of this security system. Therefore, it is difficult to estimate the annual cost of this system for providing sea line protection alone. For example, the U.S. bases in Japan that accommodate the Seventh Fleet and various air wings naturally provide for the defense of Japan. But in the event of a regional war, such as the one between Iran and Iraq that threatened the flow of oil from the Middle East to the rest of the world, the United States deployed units of the Seventh Fleet to the Indian Ocean to support U.S. naval activity in the Persian Gulf. The Seventh Fleet and other forces in Japan also protect the sea routes in the Pacific Ocean and provide a nuclear deterrence as well. Finally, the Seventh Fleet, along with other U.S. forces, serves to balance the growing power of the Soviet fleet.

If it is impossible to estimate the annual cost to maintain and replace components of the U.S. Asian-Pacific security system to protect the Asian-Pacific sea lines of communication, at least we should be able to compile a rough estimate of the annual costs for the United States to maintain that system. We have not found any such cost estimates published by the U.S. Department of

Defense, the Center for Naval Analysis, or other government agencies, although cost estimates for deploying U.S. military forces in Europe do exist. The cost estimates we present below for the Asian-Pacific security system are, therefore, provisional and subject to a considerable margin of error. We first discuss the components of this system and the items that must be estimated.

In 1986, the United States allegedly stationed military personnel in Egypt (2,500), Saudi Arabia (390), Diego Garcia (1,560), Thailand (110), Australia (300), the Philippines (15,380), Okinawa (20,770), South Korea (44,370), Japan (38,960), Guam (12,050), Johnston Atoll (120), Wake Island (?), Adak Island (?), Hawaii (?) and at bases on the west coast of the United States and the Panama Canal (?). These personnel are supplemented by the people who operate the two large Pacific fleets. In addition, the United States employs civilians of American and foreign nationality. If we assume a ratio of two civilians for each U.S. military personnel and assume annual wages and benefits of $35,000 for each U.S. military personnel and half that amount for civilian personnel, we can estimate the probable range of the annual cost for the maintenance of all personnel in this security system (Table 7.2, line 1).[5]

To use these bases and locations where U.S. military personnel are stationed in foreign areas, the United States must pay rents and user fees to the owners of that property. We cannot find a complete and accurate list of these charges, and therefore, we must rely upon conjecture and the few available figures in the public domain, such as the annual payments for U.S. bases in the Philippines (Table 7.2, line 2).

Military procurement includes the direct costs of developing, producing, and buying equipment, weapons and materials, and their replacement over cycles of ten, twenty, and thirty years.[6] Such procurements are for naval vessels, aircraft, ground forces, information gathering, etc. New equipment and weapons must be phased in at different intervals to replace older items, and research and development expenses for their development must be prorated on an annual basis. We have no precise list of all the equipment, weapon systems, and materials that must be maintained and used each year for this vast security system. Furthermore, such procurement items should be categorized according to naval, air, and ground forces (Table 7.2, lines 3–5).

Next, there are miscellaneous fixed costs such as energy, insurance, legal fees, medical services, replacement of structures, and so on for each of these bases and their locations (Table 7.2, line 6).

Finally, there is a space satellite system that provides information for designated tracking units located in different centers of this vast expanse. The costs for creating this system, replacing elements of it, and utilizing it each year are classified. Our estimate is merely a guess (Table 7.2, line 7).

Table 7.2 suggests that the annual cost for the United States to maintain the huge Asian-Pacific security system came to somewhere between $36 billion and

TABLE 7.2

ANNUAL AVERAGE COST FOR MAINTAINING THE U.S. SECURITY SYSTEM
IN ASIA AND THE PACIFIC BASIN (current U.S.$ billion)

1	U.S. military and civilian personnel	$2.0 – 9.0
2	Rents and user fees	1.0 – 2.0
3	Naval procurement	12.0 – 14.0
4	Air Force procurement	9.0 – 12.0
5	Ground force procurement	5.0 – 8.0
6	Miscellaneous costs	1.5 – 3.5
7.	U.S. space satellite system	1.0 – 1.5
	TOTAL COSTS*	36.5 – 50.0

* These estimates are subject to at least a 10 percent margin of error.

$50 billion in 1986. If we assume an annual inflation rate of around 3.5 percent over the next twenty years, the cost would more than double, to around $72 billion to $100 billion, in the year 2006.

The United States confronts the following dilemma. This complex system has been built by the United States as an integrated system managed solely by the United States. That system has provided for the peace and security of the region and helped maintain the national security of the United States as well. All the elements of the system are interrelated. If the United States should lose a base, say, in the Philippines, it would incur considerable readjustment difficulties and additional costs to ensure the system's overall ability to provide the same security benefits as in the recent past. But this system is enormously expensive to provide, and it will become more expensive in future decades. Can the United States continue to pay for this system at current cost levels if demands at home for nonmilitary needs increase each year while productivity increases only at the same rates as in recent decades? Is there some way the United States can reduce these costs without reducing the system's effectiveness?

Similarly, Japan faces a dilemma. The present Japan-United States security relationship provides for the defense of Japan, particularly the security of the sea routes so vital to Japan's economy. Japan's dependence upon this security system is enormous. Until now, Japan has never been directly involved in the maintenance of that huge system.

Therefore, both countries face serious dilemmas that their current security relationship is increasingly unable to resolve. The United States needs to find some means to reduce some of the costs of maintaining this vast security system in Asia and the Pacific, while still producing the same benefits the system has long provided. Japan needs the guarantee that its sea lines of communication will be protected for the defense of its powerful economy and dynamic society. In order to preserve the security partnership that both countries have successfully built so far, we recommend a reassessment of the security relationship. We recommend, as detailed in the final chapter, that Japan shoulder and share the responsibility for maintaining the Asian-Pacific sea lines of communication.

Notes

1. Tsuneo Akaha, "Japan's Response to Threats of Shipping Disruptions in Southeast Asia and the Middle East," *Pacific Affairs*, vol. 59, no. 2 (summer 1986), p. 256.

2 Ibid., p. 259.

3. A list of these bases can be found in Capt. John Moore (ed.), *Jane's Fighting Ships, 1987–88* (New York: Jane's Publishing, Inc., 1987), p. 697.

4. A brief description of U.S. deployment of forces in the region can be found in Research Institute for Peace and Security, Tokyo, *Asian Security 1987–88* (London: Brassey's Defense Publisher, 1987), pp. 47–48.

5. For figures on numbers of U.S. military personnel, see Ruth Leger Sivard, *World Military and Social Expenditures, 1986* (Washington: World Priorities, 1986), p. 11.

6. The costs for aircraft carriers, escort vessels, submarines, aircraft, etc. can be found in John Moore (ed.), *Jane's Fighting Ships, 1987–88*. Procurement and development costs of weapons and equipment can be found in Caspar W. Weinberger, *Report of the Secretary of Defense, Caspar W. Weinberger, to the Congress on the FY 1986 Budget, 1987 Authorized Request and FY 1986–90 Defense Program, February 4, 1985* (Washington, D.C.: Government Printing Office, 1985).

8

Reassessing the
U.S.-Japan Alliance

Our review of the U.S.-Japanese security alliance shows that complex interactions between the leaders of both countries in the early postwar period produced a constitution for Japan and a security relationship of a very special kind. Japan deferred its responsibility for defense to the United States and concentrated on promoting economic development. As Japan's security management received support from the press and public opinion, a small defense industry and a slowly expanding Self-Defense Force still made it necessary for Japan to depend upon the United States for its national security even by 1988. The United States appeared to welcome this dependency relationship in exchange for having basing rights in Japan and her support for the foreign policies of the United States.

Yet a crucial question still remains to be answered. Is the current U.S.-Japan alliance satisfactory to deal with the new challenges that have emerged within the United States in the 1980s? One line of argument now urges that the current U.S.-Japan alliance should not be altered because it is working satisfactorily. Another argument, based upon the "burden sharing" viewpoint, demands that the United States ask more from Japan. We believe both points of view are fallacious and might endanger the U.S.-Japan alliance in the near future. Most important of all, these two arguments fail to resolve the two major dilemmas for Japan and the United States that we described in the preceding chapter. We briefly rebut these two arguments and then suggest how a reassessment of the U.S.-Japan alliance might build a new partnership to resolve the two dilemmas already discussed.

Defending the Status Quo

Both the U.S. State Department and the Department of Defense have vigorously defended the current relationship between Tokyo and Washington, especially as it has evolved during the eight years of the Reagan administration.

Probably the best discussion of Japan's defense policy and how it meshed with the defense policy of the United States was made in early 1988 by James E. Auer, the special assistant for Japan in the office of the United States assistant secretary of defense.[1] Auer persuasively argued that during the 1980s Japan made important contributions to upgrading and expanding its Self-Defense Forces, an account that conforms to the evidence already presented in Chapter 6. Japan's defense programs for the periods 1986–1990 and 1991–1995 will provide Japan with a new capability to protect its territory, airspace, and a limited sea line extending between Japan and the Bonin and Okinawa islands.[2] Equally important, the Self-Defense Forces have become more integrated, share a common strategy, and have limited but designated missions in cooperation with the United States Seventh Fleet. Auer concludes that by the mid-1990s Japan's defense capability conceivably might have a "first-class, high-technology air defense, anti-submarine and anti-invasion bulwark very close to the Soviet Union."[3]

Another recent study of Japan's defense policies and buildup during the 1980s stresses that Japan did respond to requests that it do more for its security but that American policy-makers should be more sensitive and understanding of why it took the Japanese so long to modestly upgrade their defense forces. An observer of Japanese defense policy, Harry Holland, urges that "it is in our mutual interests to preserve a satisfactory security relationship; to minimize friction and tension that lap at the shores of our common concern for peace."[4] In short, such experts as Auer and Holland believe that the current U.S.-Japan alliance is a satisfactory relationship and should be nurtured in every possible way, and only greater American understanding of the behavior and psychology of the Japanese will enable both partners to maintain the current relationship. In other words, policy-makers in Washington need only modulate the U.S.-Japan security relationship in gradual ways to preserve its intrinsic features: continued Japanese dependency upon the United States for their security, with marginal improvement and expansion of the country's Self-Defense Forces.

The New Demand for Burden Sharing

American resentment toward Japan grew by leaps and bounds during the 1980s. Many charged that Japan's peculiar institutions gave it an unfair advantage in foreign trade: the practice of permanent employment, the bonus system, government industrial policies, and so forth. Pressures mounted in Washington to demand that the dollar be devalued to make Japanese imports more expensive and American exports cheaper so as to reduce the soaring trade surplus in favor of Japan. Still others asked that Japan entirely reorient its economy from export dependency toward domestic-demand dependence. And others complained about Japan's allegedly unfair, adversarial, or non-reciprocal trading practices. Such arguments, when taken together, argue for economic concessions from Japan while granting time for the United States to put its house in order to restore its former economic competitive edge.

Meanwhile, to put new teeth into these demands, the United States has resorted to trade sanctions, as in 1987, when it demanded and received a new share of Japan's semiconductor chip market. Similarly, the U.S. Treasury Department has been heavily leaning on Japan to secure an adequate level of Japanese investments for U.S. Treasury notes. While upset by these bullying arrangements, the Japanese have so far remained silent by telling themselves that this is the cost of military dependence. But how much longer can these unilateral actions by the United States take place without negative reaction in Japan becoming so strong as to rupture the U.S.-Japan alliance and push Japan in a new direction not unlike that which took place after the Anglo-Japanese alliance was terminated in 1921? Most assuredly, we should not allow that to happen again, for if it does, Japan may become a true military threat to the United States.

And yet America's sense of dissatisfaction with Japan is not unfounded, because Japan has recently challenged the United States in the realm of production and distribution. Japan's ability to mount this economic challenge is closely connected with the long-term security alliance with the United States, which Washington has vigorously tried to maintain. By keeping the alliance without Japan reciprocating more for defense, the trade dispute between the two partners seems to have worsened. Japan is now damned for a military free ride and damned as well if it acts too vigorously on behalf of its security.

Let's examine the linkage between America's economic woes and its defense policy for the 1980s. The United States had a trade surplus in its current account in 1980, although quite small. Confronted with the Soviet invasion of Afghanistan and by a widely perceived shift in the military balance to favor the Soviet Union, the Reagan administration pursued military expansion that was financed by a tremendous budget deficit. Refusing to raise taxes to finance greater defense spending, the Reagan administration demanded that Congress cut back spending. Congressional refusal to reduce spending collided with stubborn administration resistance to raise taxes, and so the great budget deficit ballooned, with members of each political party accusing the other of irrational policies and unreasonable political behavior.

Meanwhile, Japanese investors found it profitable to cover part of this deficit, and quite naturally Japan paid for its capital export out of its mounting trade surplus with the United States. Japan's ability to penetrate U.S. markets had greatly increased in the 1980s, representing the culmination of more than a decade of learning how to produce and market products for the high-income segments of the U.S. market. At the same time, many years of bad management, rising costs, and failure to innovate had left many American manufacturing industries extremely vulnerable to foreign competition. In the 1980s, American manufacturing contracted, followed by loud cries from labor, capital, and other interest groups for protection from the alleged unfair trading practices of foreign producers. The end result was that more and more American policy-makers began to blame Japan for the country's economic dilemmas while pointing to the fact that Japan paid so little for its defense.

To deal with these new problems, the powers in Washington now seem to insist that the United States must maintain its military presence in the Pacific Basin but that its ally, Japan, should pay more of the bill. The U.S. House of Representatives has already passed a resolution calling for the annual levy of a sum equivalent to 1 percent of Japan's gross national product, which would amount to roughly $30 billion. Some maintain that Japan should be subject to such a levy and Europe should remain exempt, without showing how such discrimination would be justified.[5] Another form of burden sharing with Japan is to request a large-scale Japanese Marshall Plan. To this end, the *New York Times* has called for the Japanese to underwrite the Third World debt to U.S. banks.[6] These new demands on Japan have been rationalized by the new argument that if Japan can spend more to aid developing countries, Japan and the United States will somehow become more interconnected in their international financial commitments and interests. In this way, argues Zbigniew Brzezinski, a new two-country amalgam one might call "Amerinippon" will emerge.[7] But Brzezinski does not ask how Nippon can be asked to be the tail of America and make a huge outlay of its financial resources all at the same time. Is it not reasonable to expect Nippon to demand something in return for a Marshall Plan or to refuse the request out of hand?

How to Damage the U.S.-Japan Alliance

Japan already has made impressive advances to increase foreign assistance to developing countries. In 1979, Japan contributed only around $1.47 billion to Indonesia, Malaysia, the Philippines, South Korea, and Thailand, but in 1985 she had increased that amount to $3.17 billion to include the People's Republic of China as well.[8] By 1992, Japan will have doubled foreign aid to developing countries by more than $50 billion, to exceed the aid given by any other country.[9]

Because Japan has long been responding to demands from Washington to spend more for defense, purchase U.S. Treasury debt instruments, and provide economic aid to developing countries, there is something bullying and insidious in Washington insensitively demanding that Tokyo do more for burden sharing. In fact, "burden sharing" is an improper term to formulate foreign policy toward one's close ally, particularly when the ally has always complied with all previous American demands; but Washington now demands burden sharing from a close ally, especially an ally who has been placed in a position of subordination and dependency for nearly four decades. We argue that this approach is simply not the way to manage U.S. security interests in Asia and the Pacific with so important an ally as Japan.

The simple fact of the matter is that demanding that Japan undertake greater defense burden sharing while not granting Japan an equal partnership in maintaining the security of Asia and the Pacific Basin is bound to erode Japanese goodwill. Moreover, Japan's current defense spending and cooperation with the United States defense forces in that region are inadequate to deal with the two major dilemmas that already face both countries.

We have argued that the United States must annually pay a huge sum of money to maintain the large security system it has maintained for over forty years in Asia and the Pacific region. At the same time, Japan and the other Asian and Pacific countries and territories are heavily dependent upon sea lines for commerce. These two dilemmas are not adequately resolved by the current defense program supported by the U.S. Departments of State and Defense and by Japan's leaders. Why?

It appears very unlikely that the United States can continue to spend in the vicinity of $40 billion to $50 billion annually for the upkeep of the Pacific-Asian security network unless defense spending in other parts of the world is reduced or more resources can be allocated for defense in the United States budget. A large reallocation for its Asian and Pacific security commitments by the United States is unlikely in the near future. Meanwhile, powerful pressures within the United States are mounting to reduce defense spending rather than sustain it at previous levels.

Although the United States enjoyed considerable economic prosperity in the past eight years as employment expanded and productivity picked up slightly compared to the 1970s, the United States economy appears to be in a transition period of relative economic decline compared to many other economies.[10] The U.S. ratio of savings to gross national product is at its lowest level since the late 1940s; major industries that provided the United States with the ability to project military power are now in decline, largely because of plunging corporate profits and numerous enterprises exiting from those industries; widespread pockets of poverty have become visible; a sharp jump in the inequality of income distribution has been viewed by many with alarm and disappointment. These and other indicators of economic change in the 1980s suggest that the economy of the United States is a mixture of successes and serious problems. Therefore, it is highly questionable that the United States can continue to meet its security commitments in various parts of the globe in the coming decade unless its economy can be revitalized.

Meanwhile, the danger to sea lines for the Asian-Pacific states and territories remains the same. Regional wars such as the decade-long conflict between Iraq and Iran in the Persian Gulf still threaten vital supplies of energy for Asia and the Pacific region. The Soviet Union still maintains a powerful naval presence in the Pacific region and now matches the naval power and air force capability of the United States. The People's Republic of China is using its resources to build up a modern navy, which in the near future could be projected into various areas of the Pacific Basin. But these two major dilemmas can be resolved by reassessing the U.S.-Japan security alliance.

Reassessing the Alliance

The responsible agencies in both the Japanese and United States governments can consult to develop a new military partnership for the Pacific Basin. This new partnership would be based upon equality and true reciprocity in terms of the maintenance of the national security of both countries. The new military partnership would be based upon an arrangement similar to that which has long existed in Europe under NATO. United States and Japanese defense forces would cooperate to monitor and protect the sea routes of communication at a distance of 5,000 km from Japan. That distance would extend from Tokyo to Singapore, from Tokyo nearly to Hawaii, and nearly three-quarters of the distance from Tokyo to Vancouver.[11]

Such cooperation could enable the United States to reduce some of its costs for regional security and still provide a firm commitment to protect the sea lines of communication so vital to Japan and the rest of the region. How could this be done?

Japan would have to acquire the naval and air force capability to take on the mission of providing part of the sea route defense up to 5,000 kilometers. Rather than have Japan's defense industry produce that new defense capability, a specific number of aircraft carriers, escort vessels, minesweepers, submarines, air wings, and so on from the U.S. Seventh Fleet could be transferred to Japan for an agreed-upon sum. The military experts of both countries could agree to those numbers and the price. Meanwhile, the United States would shift to a single, large fleet with support forces to provide for the security of the Pacific. But a small component of that fleet would cooperate under a NATO-type arrangement with our Japanese ally, whose Self-Defense Forces would have been enlarged by acquiring a substantial portion of the U.S. Seventh Fleet. This new NATO-style defense force would have the same mission that the Seventh Fleet now performs: providing for the security of the northeast Pacific.[12] At the same time, U.S.-Japan defense forces would deploy some units to the Indian Ocean when security conditions dictated. Finally, the United States would have a single, large naval fleet with support forces to represent an enlarged U.S. Third Fleet.

We can only guess at the possible savings for the United States during a transition period that might take as long as a decade to complete. Such savings might commence at as little as $3 billion to $4 billion per year, with savings accumulating rapidly and perhaps amounting to as much as $30 billion to $40 billion over the course of a decade. The money saved could then be allocated to the U.S. economy and society. Moreover, the United States would receive additional proceeds from the sale of part of the Seventh Fleet to Japan.

Meanwhile, Japan would develop a new defense force capability commensurate with its economic power and diplomatic responsibilities in the region. While cooperating closely with the United States in the northeast and western Pacific, Japan would be able to protect the vital sea routes of communication to the outside world that she and her neighbors so greatly depend upon.[13] This new U.S.-Japan security relationship would not threaten other countries of the region. It would represent a momentous step forward for allied cooperation in the region.

Notes

1. James E. Auer, "Japan's Defense Policy," *Current History*, vol. 87, no. 528 (April 1988), pp. 145–148 and 180–182.

2. Ibid., p. 181.

3. Ibid., p. 182.

4. Harrison M. Holland, *Managing Defense: Japan's Dilemma* (Lanham, Md.: University Press of America, 1988), p. 65.

5. James Chace, "Ike Was Right," *Atlantic Monthly*, August 1987, pp. 39–41.

6. "It's America's Debt Crisis, Too," *New York Times* (editorial), February 29, 1988, p. 37.

7. "America's New Geostrategy," *Foreign Affairs*, spring 1988, pp. 680–699.

8. Juichi Inada, "Japan's Aid Diplomacy: Increasing Role for Global Security," *Japan Review of International Affairs*, vol. 2, no. 1 (spring/summer 1988), p. 97. The original figures are in current yen values, and they have been converted into U.S. dollars at the exchange rate of ¥125 = U.S. $1.

9. Patrick L. Smith, "Japan Is Doubling, to $50 Billion, Aid to Developing Countries," *International Herald Tribune*, June 15, 1988, p. 2.

10. See Emma Rothschild, "The Real Reagan Economy," *New York Review of Books*, June 30, 1988, pp. 46–53. While we do not concur with all of the author's negative evaluations of U.S. economic development during the Reagan administration, we believe that the evidence cited from U.S. government economic reports shows the glaring weaknesses of the U.S. economy, thereby reflecting its relative economic decline as compared to other advanced countries.

11. The distance between Tokyo and Singapore is 5,321 km, and between Tokyo and Honolulu 6,202 km. See Gerard Chaliand and Jean-Pierre Rageau, *Strategic Atlas: A Comparative Geopolitics of the World's Powers* (New York: Harper & Row, 1985), p. 218.

12. A rough estimate of the number of naval ships, air wings, and military

manpower making up the U.S. Seventh Fleet and the U.S. forces deployed in the Indian Ocean can be found in International Institute for Strategic Studies, *The Military Balance, 1986–1987* (London: International Institute for Strategic Studies, 1986), pp. 28–30.

13. Ordinary Japanese citizens would very likely welcome this new defense partnership and take pride in Japan's recovery of its defense responsibility. For one such reaction, see the interview with Hyuga Hosai, "Shouldering of Share of Defense Costs in Persian Gulf Is Natural," *Summaries of Selected Japanese Magazines,* January 1988, p. 8.

Bibliography

Books

Barnett, Robert W. *Beyond War: Japan's Concept of Comprehensive National Security*. Washington: Pergamon Press, 1984.

Calleo, David P. *Beyond American Hegemony: The Future of the Western Alliance*. New York: Basic Books, 1987.

Chūma, Kiyofuku. *Saigunbi no seiji-gaku* [Politics of Rearmament]. Tokyo: Chishikisha, 1985.

Council of Economic Advisers. *Economic Report of the President: Transmitted to the Congress February 1988*. Washington, D.C.: Government Printing Office, 1988.

Defense Agency. *Defense of Japan, 1986*. Tokyo: Japan Times, 1986.

————. *Defense of Japan, 1987*. Tokyo: Japan Times, 1987.

Dower, John W. *Empire and Aftermath: Yoshida Shigeru and the Japanese Experience, 1878–1954*. Cambridge, Mass.: Harvard University Press, 1979.

Funabashi, Yōichi. *Tsūka retsu retsu* [Currency War]. Tokyo: Asahi Shimbunsha, 1988.

Hata, Ikuhiko. *Shiroku saigunbi* [History of Rearmament]. Tokyo: Bungei Shunjūsha, 1976.

Holland, Harrison M. *Managing Defense: Japan's Dilemma*. (Lanham, Md.: University Press of America, 1988).

Igarashi, Takeshi. *Tai-Nichi kōwa to reisen: sengo Nichi-Bei kankei no keisei* [Peace with Japan and the Cold War: The Formation of Postwar Japan-U.S. Relations]. Tokyo: Tokyo University Press, 1986.

Inoki, Masamichi, and Kōsaka, Masataka (eds.). *Nihon no anzen hoshō to bōei eno kinkyū teigen* [Some Urgent Proposals for the Security of Japan and Its Defenses]. Tokyo: Kōdansha, 1982.

James, D. Clayton. *The Years of MacArthur*, Vol. III: *Triumph and Disaster, 1945–1964*. New York: Houghton Mifflin, 1985.

Kataoka, Tetsuya. *The Price of a Constitution: The Origin of Japan's Postwar Politics* (unpublished manuscript).

Katō, Yōzō. *Shiroku Jieitai-shi* [A Biographical History of the Self-Defense Forces]. Tokyo: Gekkan Seisaku, 1979.

Keidanren, Defense Production Committee. *Defense Production in Japan*. Tokyo: Keidanren, 1985.

Keizai Koho Center. *Japan 1988: An International Comparison*. Tokyo: Japan Institute for Social and Economic Affairs, 1987.

Kennedy, Paul. *The Rise and Fall of the Great Empires: Economic Change and Military Conflict from 1500 to 2000.* New York: Random House, 1987.

Kim, Young C. *Japanese Journalists and Their World.* Charlottesville, Va.: University Press of Virginia, 1981.

Kōdansha. *Kōdansha Encyclopedia of Japan.* Tokyo: Kōdansha Ltd., 1983.

Linder, Staffan Burenstam. *The Pacific Century: Economic and Political Consequences of Asian-Pacific Dynamism.* Stanford, Calif.: Stanford University Press, 1986.

Maki, John M. (ed.). *Conflict and Tension in the Far East: Key Documents, 1894–1960.* Seattle: University of Washington Press, 1961.

Miyazawa, Kiichi. *Tokyo-Washinton no mitsudan* [Secret Talks Between Tokyo and Washington]. Tokyo: Jitsugyō no Nihonsha, 1956.

Moore, John (ed.). *Jane's Fighting Ships, 1987–88.* New York: Jane's Publishing, Inc., 1987.

Murakami, Yasusuke, et al. *Bunmei to shite no ie shakai* [The Ie-Society as a Civilization]. Tokyo: Chūō Kōronsha, 1985.

NHK Hōsō yoron chōsajo (ed.). *Zusetsu: sengo yoron shi* [A History of Postwar Public Opinion in Diagram]. Tokyo: NKH Books, 1982.

Nagao, Ryūichi (ed.). *Nihon kempōshi* [History of Japan's Constitutions]. Tokyo: Tokyo University Press, 1976.

Nihon Shimbun Kyōkai. *The Japanese Press, 1983.* Tokyo: Japan Newspaper Publishers' and Editors' Association, 1983.

Ogawa, Kazuhisa. *Zai Nichi Bei gun* [U.S. Forces in Japan]. Tokyo: Kōdansha, 1985.

Okazaki, Hisahiko. *Senryaku-teki shikō towa nanika* [What Is Strategic Thinking?]. Tokyo: Chūō Kōronsha, 1983.

Olsen, Edward A. *U.S.-Japan Strategic Reciprocity: A New Internationalist View.* Stanford, Calif.: Hoover Institution Press, 1985.

Ōtake, Hideo. *Adenauaa to Yoshida Shigeru* [Adenauer and Shigeru Yoshida]. Tokyo: Chūō Kōronsha, 1986.

————. *Nihon no bōei to kokunai seiji* [Japan's Defense and Domestic Politics]. Tokyo: Sanichi Shobō, 1983.

Prestowitz, Clyde V., Jr. *Trading Places: How We Allowed Japan to Take the Lead.* New York: Basic Books, 1988.

Research Institute for Peace and Security, Tokyo. *Asian Security, 1987–88.* London: Brassey's Defense Publisher, 1987.

Sivard, Ruth Leger. *World Military and Social Expenditures, 1986.* Washington: World Priorities, 1986.

Solomon, Richard H., and Kosaka, Masataka (eds.). *The Soviet Far East Military Buildup: Nuclear Dilemmas and Asian Security.* Dover, Mass.: Auburn House Publishing Company, 1986.

Sōrifu [Prime Minister's Office] (ed.). *Yoron chōsa* [A Survey of Public Opinion]. Tokyo: Sōrifu, 1985.

Tomiyama, Kazuo. *Nihon no bōei sangyō* [Japan's Defense Industry]. Tokyo: Toyo Keizai Shimpōsha, 1979.

U.S. State Department. *Foreign Relations of the United States, 1951.*

Washington, D.C.: Government Printing Office, 1980, VI, Pt. 1.

Weinberger, Caspar W. *Report of the Secretary of Defense, Caspar W. Weinberger, to the Congress on the FY 1986 Budget, 1987 Authorized Request and FY 1986–90 Defense Program, February 4, 1985*. Washington, D.C.: Government Printing Office, 1985.

Yoshida, Shigeru. *Sekai to Nihon* [The World and Japan]. Tokyo: Banchō Shobō, 1963.

Articles

Akaha, Tsuneo. "Japan's Response to Threats of Shipping Disruptions in Southeast Asia and the Middle East," *Pacific Affairs,* summer 1986, pp. 256–266.

Auer, James A. "Japan's Defense Policy," *Current History,* April 1988, pp. 145–149.

Bernstein, Alvin H. "The Soviets in Cam Ranh Bay," *The National Interest,* Spring 1986, pp. 17–29.

Brzezinski, Zbigniew. "America's New Geostrategy," *Foreign Affairs,* spring 1988, pp. 680–699.

Buruma, Ian. "A New Japanese Nationalism," *New York Times Magazine,* April 12, 1987, pp. 15–24.

Calder, Kent E. "Japanese Foreign Economic Policy Formation: Explaining the Reactive State," *World Politics,* forthcoming.

Chace, James. "Ike Was Right," *The Atlantic Monthly,* August 1987, pp. 39–41.

Fukuda, Takeo. "Senzen no kurai michi o ayundewa naranai" [Don't Walk the Dark Prewar Path], *Ekonomisuto,* October 8, 1985, pp. 24–29.

Gunji Kagaku Kenkyukai. "Nihon ga motsubeki bōeiryoku" [The Defense Power Japan Ought To Have], *Shokun,* July 1980, part II, pp. 68–104.

Huntington, Samuel P. "Coping with the Lippman Gap," *Foreign Affairs,* spring 1988, pp. 453–477.

Igarashi, Takeshi. "Heiwa no kōsō: shin no kokusaiteki sekinin towa nanika" [The Concept of Peace: What Is Our True International Responsibility?], *Sekai,* April 1985, pp. 27–42.

Inoki, Masamichi. "Bōei rongi no kyojitsu" [The Truth and Fallacies of the Defense Controversy], *Chūō Kōron,* January 1981, pp. 110–120.

——. "Soren no 'kyōi' ni dō taisho suruka" [How To Cope with the Soviet Threat], *Chūō Kōron,* November 1976, pp. 56–65.

Kaihara, Osamu, et al. "This Is Japan's Defense Power," *Shūkan Yomiuri,* March 5, 1978, cited in *Summaries of Selected Japanese Magazines (SSJM),* translated by the Political Section of the American Embassy, Tokyo, March 1978, p. 33.

Kase, Hideaki. "Nihon rettō no bōei seimeisen" [The Defense Lifeline of the Japanese Archipelago], *Jiyū,* January 1979, pp. 18–25.

Kato, Kōichi. "Bōei shomondai no kontei ni hisomu mono" [Factors Hidden at the Roots of the Various Defense Problems], *Bungei Shunjū,* August 1985, pp. 194–199.

Kilborn, Peter T. "Key U.S. Shift Seen to Job Protection from Free Trade," *New York Times,* April 29, 1988, p. 1.

Kitamura, Kenichi. "Shirein bōeiron" [An Essay on the Defense of the Sea Lanes], presented to the Special Committee on Security of the Upper House of the Diet Discussing the Problems and Characteristics of the Defense of the Sea Lanes (April 11, 1983).

————. "Taiheiyō shīrein no anzen hoshō to kokusai kyōryoku" [International Cooperation and the Security of the Pacific Sea Lanes], *Sekai to Nihon*, December 25, 1983, pp. 8–49.

Komori, Yoshihisa. "The Role of the Press in Japanese Government Decision-Making on Defense" (a draft copy of a prepared statement to a workshop sponsored by the House Foreign Affairs Committee, Subcommittee on Asian and Pacific Affairs; the Woodrow Wilson International Center for Scholars; and the Congressional Research Service).

Kondō, Koichi, and Komori, Yoshihisa. "Nihonjin kisha no kokusai kankaku" [The International Sense of Japanese Reporters], *Bungei Shunjū*, November 1983, pp. 328–340.

Kraar, Louis. "The New Powers of Asia," *Fortune*, March 28, 1988, pp. 126–132.

Kubo, Takuya. "Kokubō kaigi no kyōka o" [Strengthening the National Defense Council], *Ekonomisuto*, February 15, 1977, pp. 40–43.

Maruyama, Hiroyuki. "Soren Taiheiyō kantai o keikai seyo" [Take Heed of the Soviet Pacific Fleet], *Shokun*, November 1985, pp. 97–105.

Miyazawa, Kiichi, and Kosaka, Masataka. "Watashi no shisan baizōron—dai niji keizai hiyaku to heiwa kyōryoku gaikō" [My Plank for Doubling Property: The Second Economic Leap and the Diplomacy of Peaceful Cooperation], *Bungei Shunjū*, July 1984, pp. 94–114.

Miyoshi, Osamu. "Chūritsu Nihon ka, shin Nichi-Bei dōmei ka" [A Neutral Japan or a New Japan-U.S. Alliance?], *Chūō Kōron*, March 1980, pp. 92–108.

Momoi, Makoto. "Nihon no 'sōgō' anzen hoshō o kangaeru: 80-nendai ni nami takamaru Taiheiyō eno taiō" [Considering Japan's 'Comprehensive' Security: Coping with the Pacific as the Waves Mount Higher in the 1980s], *Keieisha*, August, 1979, pp. 28–33.

Nagai, Yōnosuke. "Moratoriamu kokka no bōeiron" [The Defense Debate of the Moratorium State], *Chūō Kōron*, January 1981, pp. 74–108.

————. "Nihon gaikō ni okeru 'shizen' to 'sakui'" [Naturalness and Artificiality in Japan's Diplomacy], *Chūō Kōron*, June 1982, pp. 72–93.

Nakagawa, Yatsuhiro. "Kaku no mochikomi igai no michi wa nai" [There Is No Other Way Except To Have a Nuclear Power Introduced], *Shokun*, September 1980, pp. 62–85.

Nakamura, Kenichi. "Soren kyōiron kara no dakkyakyu" [Extricating Ourselves from the Thesis of Soviet Threat], *Sekai*, April 1985, pp. 56–73.

Nihon heiki kōgyōkai [Japanese Military Weapons Industry Association]. "Buki seisan kōzō chōsa" [A Survey of the Structure of Weapons Production], in *Kikai kōgyō kiso chōsa* [Basic Survey of the Machine Industry], no. 4, pp. 98–99.

Nishimura, Shigeki. "Developing Outlook on Soviet Moves, the Soviet Union, and Substance of Potential Threat: Epoch-Making Discussion Clarifying Ambiguous Argument on Soviet Threat," *Summaries of Selected Japanese Magazines*, December 1985, p. 8.

————. "Nihon no bōei senryaku o kangaeru: gurōbaru-apurōchi ni yoru hoppō zenpō bōei-ron" [Thinking About Japan's Defense Strategy: The Forward Defense of the North Through a Global Approach], *Shin Bōei Ronshū*, July 1984, pp. 50–79.

Okazaki, Hisahiko. "Ima koso jimae no senryaku teki shikō o" [Now Is the Time for Our Own Strategic Thought], *Bungei Shunjū*, March 1986, pp. 110–126.

————. "Magarikado ni kita Nichi-Bei dōmei [The Japan-U.S. Alliance at a Crossroad], *Bungei Shunjū*, July 1988, pp. 94–111.

————."Nihon bōei no tame no kihon senryaku" [The Basic Strategy for Defending Japan], *Voice*, September 1983, pp. 64–81.

Okimiya, Masataka. "Sōgō anzen hoshō eno teigen" [A Proposal for a Comprehensive Security], *Shin Bōei Ronshū*, March 1974, pp. 1–22.

Ōkita, Saburō. "Time for a Japanese Marshall Plan?" *Look Japan*, January 10, 1986, pp. 2–3.

Ōmura, Jōji, and Etō, Shinkichi. "80 nendai no bōei mondai ni dō taiō suruka" [How To Deal with the Defense Problem of the 1980s?], *Bungei Shunjū*, November 1980, pp. 368–375.

Schmeisser, Peter. "Taking Stock: Is America in Decline?" *New York Times Magazine*, April 17, 1988, pp. 24–96.

Sentō, Masaaki. "Nihon wa 'gakuwari kokka' de aru: tenki no Nichi-Bei bōei masatsu o kangeru" [Japan Is a Dependent State: A Review of Japan-U.S. Defense Friction at a Turning Point], *Jiyū*, October 1983, pp. 102–109.

Shimizu, Ikutarō. "Kaku no sentaku: Nihon yo kokka tare" [The Nuclear Option: Japan, Be a State!], *Shokun*, July 1980, pp. 22–68.

Silk, Leonard. "Proposals to Keep the U.S. on Top," *New York Times*, April 1, 1988, p. 28(Y).

Stokes, Henry Scott. "Lost Samurai: The Withered Soul of Postwar Japan," *Harpers*, October 1985, pp. 55–62.

Tomiyama, Kazuo. "Weapons Manufacturers Continue to Grow," *Japan Quarterly*, July/September 1982, pp. 335–345.

van Wolferen, Karel G. "The Japan Problem," *Foreign Affairs*, Winter 1986/87, pp. 288–303.

White, Theodore H. "The Danger from Japan," *New York Times Magazine*, July 28, 1985, pp. 7–43.

Yamazaki, Takio. "Jiyū to dokuritsu o mamoru bōeiryoku" [Defense Power for Preserving Freedom and Independence], *Jiyū*, December 1980, pp. 113–123.

————. "'Kekkan' jieitai to shiteki sarete" [The Self-Defense Forces Have Been Singled Out as Defective], *Jiyū*, August 1980, pp. 65–71.

————. "Nihon no anzen o dō iji suruka" [How To Maintain Japan's Security?], *Jiyū*, May 1980, pp. 127–132.

Yasuhara, Kazuo. "Dare ga futan surunoka" [Who Bears the Burden?], *Sekai*, November 1985, pp. 70–80.

Periodicals

Embassy of the United States, Tokyo. *Daily Summary of Japanese Press*.
————. *Summaries of Selected Japanese Magazines*.

Index